Web Design Before & After Makeovers™

WILEY
Wiley Publishing, Inc.

By
Richard Wagner

Web Design Before & After Makeovers™

Published by
Wiley Publishing, Inc.
111 River Street
Hoboken, NJ 07030-5774
www.wiley.com

For general information on our other products and services, please contact our Customer Care Department within the U.S. at 800-762-2974, outside the U.S. at 317-572-3993, or fax 317-572-4002.

For technical support, please visit www.wiley.com/techsupport.

Wiley also publishes its books in a variety of electronic formats. Some content that appears in print may not be available in electronic books.

Library of Congress Control Number: 2006920619

ISBN-13: 978-0-471-78323-7

ISBN-10: 0-471-78323-4

Manufactured in the United States of America

10 9 8 7 6 5 4 3 2 1

1K/RY/QU/QW/IN

WILEY

Meet the Author

Richard Wagner is an experienced Web designer and author of several Web technology books, including *Yahoo SiteBuilder For Dummies, XSLT For Dummies, XML All-in-One Desk Reference For Dummies,* and *JavaScript Unleashed.* He is the former Vice President of Product Development at NetObjects and inventor of the award-winning NetObjects ScriptBuilder Web tool. In his non-tech life, Richard is also author of *C.S. Lewis & Narnia For Dummies, Christianity For Dummies,* and *The Gospel Unplugged.* His online home is at Digitalwalk.com.

Author's Acknowledgments

Special thanks go to Steve Hayes, for giving me the opportunity to work on this book project; Paul Levesque, for your direction and guidance throughout the process; Andy Hollandbeck, for your editing feedback and suggestions; and Dennis Cohen, for your keen attention to the technical details throughout the book.

Dedication

To Kimberly

Publisher's Acknowledgments

We're proud of this book; please send us your comments at www.wiley.com/.

Some of the people who helped bring this book to market include the following:

Acquisitions, Editorial, and Media Development

Senior Project Editor: **Paul Levesque**

Acquisitions Editor: **Steve Hayes**

Copy Editor: **Andy Hollandbeck**

Technical Editor: **Dennis Cohen**

Editorial Manager: **Leah P. Cameron**

Media Development Manager: **Laura VanWinkle**

Media Development Supervisor: **Richard Graves**

Editorial Assistant: **Amanda Foxworth**

Composition Services

Book Designer: **LeAndra Hosier**

Project Coordinator: **Adrienne Martinez**

Layout and Graphics: **Lauren Goddard, Denny Hager, Heather Ryan**

Proofreaders: **Debbye Butler, Jessica Kramer**

Indexer: **Rebecca R. Plunkett**

Publishing and Editorial for Technology Dummies

Richard Swadley, Vice President and Executive Group Publisher

Andy Cummings, Vice President and Publisher

Mary Bednarek, Executive Acquisitions Director

Mary C. Corder, Editorial Director

Publishing for Consumer Dummies

Diane Graves Steele, Vice President and Publisher

Joyce Pepple, Acquisitions Director

Composition Services

Gerry Fahey, Vice President of Production Services

Debbie Stailey, Director of Composition Services

Table of Contents

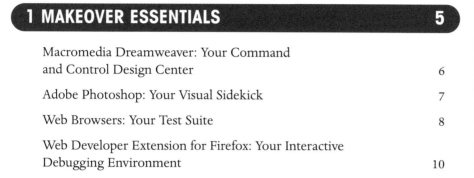

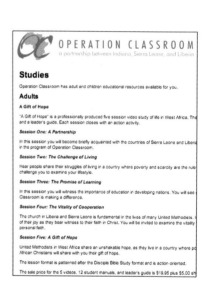

vi   Table of Contents

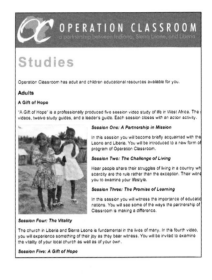

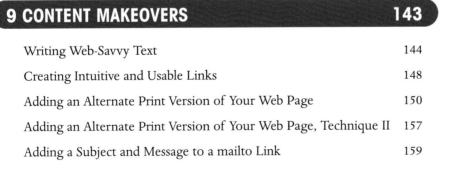

Introduction

The Metamorphosis. The Transformation. The Makeover.

From fairy tales to Walt Disney cartoons to diet pill ads to home improvement television shows, we all have a natural interest in witnessing change taking place before our eyes. The ugly duckling becomes the swan. The neglected step-sister is transformed into a gorgeous beauty at the prince's ball. The rundown house is made over into the jewel of the neighborhood. When we see these metamorphoses happening to others, we are inspired to emulate these same kinds of changes in our lives.

This desire for transformation extends into cyberspace as well. You create or maintain a Web site that you put a lot of work into, but you see how poorly it compares to other sites you visit on the Internet. You realize that what your Web site really needs is a makeover.

Before & After Makeover: The Concept

Web Design Before & After Makeovers is written to enable you to make over your Web site. With this book, you get a chance to work with dozens of mini-projects that parallel the sorts of improvements you'll encounter as you revamp and overhaul the design of your Web site. These challenges include such tasks as making your home page a compelling place that visitors will want to bookmark and return to often, placing great content on your pages without cramming it in, making your site easy and intuitive to navigate, and ensuring your pages load blazingly fast.

How to Get Around in This Book

The makeovers contained in the book are divided into 12 distinct areas. Here's a chapter-by-chapter overview of what you can expect:

Chapter 1: Makeover Essentials

In this initial chapter, you explore the tools that you'll use to perform your Web site makeovers. These software essentials include Macromedia Dreamweaver (or another HTML editor), Adobe Photoshop (or another image editor), a full set of browsers, and a really nifty debugging tool.

Chapter 2: Page Layout Makeovers

This chapter explores the physical layout of a Web page, examining how to size and arrange content on the page. You also look at how to center your pages within the browser.

Chapter 3: Navigation Makeovers

In this chapter, you focus on the challenge of making your site easy to navigate, whether it has 5, 50, or 500 pages. You look at how to create top and sidebar navigation using CSS and a drop-down combo box for quick links.

Chapter 4: Page Element Makeovers

You get to dive into the design of the elements you place on a page in this chapter. Tables and their borders are looked at first; then you examine how to space elements so that they coexist well on a page. Finally, iframes are explored as a great way to package content on your site.

Chapter 5: Text Makeovers

Communication is the *raison d'être* for the Web, so text is arguably the most important element on your Web pages. And yet, *how* you present that textual information is often even more important than the content itself. This chapter examines how to work with typefaces and font sizes by using CSS. It then focuses on how you can use text as an image to present page headings, headlines, or other eye-grabbing needs.

Chapter 6: Image Makeovers

This chapter shows you how to give your Web site a face-lift by improving the way you use images on it. You explore how to create an image rollover, crop an image, and create thumbnail images. And, if you need to display several images on a single page, be sure to check out the Image Scroller makeover in this chapter.

Chapter 7: Image Performance Makeovers

Just having nice images on your Web site is not enough. Unless they are small enough to be downloaded quickly, no one will stick around long enough to see your wonderwork. Therefore, in this chapter, you explore tricks that shorten your image download time without losing image quality.

Chapter 8: Home Page Makeovers

In this chapter, you focus on transforming your Web site's most important page — the home page. You look at how to target the content of your page for the type of visitors who come to it. You also explore how to make your home page come alive with fresh, dynamic content.

Chapter 9: Content Makeovers

While much of the book's focus is on the design and look of the Web site, this chapter looks at makeovers of your site's content. You discover how to transform the content of your Web site to better communicate with your visitors. Also, explore how to write Web-savvy text, how to place links in the best locations, and how to add alternate printable versions of your pages.

Chapter 10: Form Makeovers

Forms are often one of the ugliest parts of a Web site. Discover in this chapter how you can use CSS to enhance the look of any form as well as replace normal HTML buttons with graphical buttons. You also explore how to use JavaScript to validate your forms before they are submitted to the server.

Chapter 11: Add-On Makeovers

This chapter shows you how to use various add-ons to increase the functionality of your site's offerings. Explore how to add maps, directions, a site search feature, and a blog page.

Chapter 12: Site Makeovers

This chapter examines makeovers that impact your whole site. You look at how to link to other sites without losing your visitors. Then you find out how to create your own Favorites icon. Finally, you discover how to make over your Web site to maximize your search engine ranking.

Chapter 13: Extreme Makeovers

It's time to get radical in the final chapter. You explore how to perform some extreme makeovers that will transform your site into something state-of-the-art. Check out how to let your visitors control the size of the font on your site and how to customize the content based on the type of visitor. Finally, add the latest technology — RSS feeds — to your Web site to better communicate with your visitors.

Essential Makeover Tools

The makeovers covered in this book are written specifically for our recommended tools of choice: Macromedia Dreamweaver and Adobe Photoshop. However, the makeovers are designed to be flexible enough to be performed using most any HTML editor and image software.

Companion Web Site

Many of the makeovers covered in the book have accompanying HTML or image files that you can work with to more easily follow along with the makeover instructions. If you want to download these files, go to `www.wiley.com/go/makeovers`.

Your Invitation to Participate!

After you've had a chance to use the makeovers in this book on your Web site, I invite you to come up with your own. If you come up with something that you think would be helpful to others and would like to share it, feel free to send it to us at `makeovers@digitalwalk.net`. I might select it for use in another edition of *Web Design Before & After Makeovers*.

Before

After

1

MAKEOVER ESSENTIALS

Almost all those household makeovers you see on TV are within the realm of the possible, given a little know-how and the right tools. *Web Design Before & After Makeovers* is going to help equip you with the information you need to successfully make over your Web site. But you'll want to be sure to gather the right tools for the job before you start.

In this chapter, you explore the essential software tools that you need for getting the most from your makeovers. These tools help you design, lay out, and manage your Web site, create textual and graphical content to place on it, and test and debug your pages. While many quality software applications can handle these sorts of jobs, here are my recommendations as you assemble tools for your Web makeover toolbox. These are the tools I swear by for all of my Web design work.

Macromedia Dreamweaver: Your Command and Control Design Center

Let Macromedia Dreamweaver (or a comparable alternative tool) serve as your "command and control" center throughout your Web site design and development process.

Available for both Mac and Windows, Dreamweaver's integrated design environment packs in all of the page-design and site-management accessories you need with a mouse click.

A powerful Web page editor is crucial to performing great makeovers. After all, whether you are working with textual or graphical content, Cascading Stylesheets (CSS), JavaScript code, or DHTML, when all is said and done, you are always working with an HTML file. Dreamweaver sports a powerful page-design environment that allows you to work with a page visually and on the underlying code itself.

However, in addition to page editing, Dreamweaver helps you manage your entire Web site and its assets.

Alternatives

Microsoft FrontPage is a secondary option that some Windows users may prefer, especially for those experienced Microsoft Office product users.

No matter what tool you use, opt for a tool that provides both visual and code views of the Web page and that has the site support features you need as you design pages.

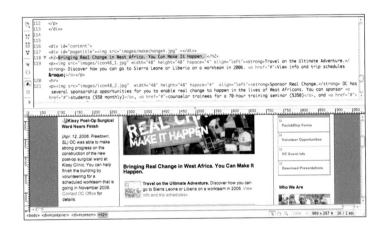

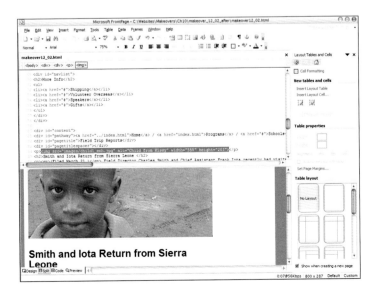

Adobe Photoshop: Your Visual Sidekick

Nice-looking, optimized graphics are an essential component to nearly every well-designed, professional-caliber Web site. As such, even if you don't consider yourself a graphic artist, you'll still want to opt for a professional-grade image editor. The hands-down winner in this category is Adobe Photoshop. Even though you may use only a small percentage of its expansive functionality, Photoshop is well worth the time and monetary investment you'll spend in order to get quality results for your Web site.

Photoshop and its trusty sidekick ImageReady handle all of the essential image-related tasks you need to perform with your Web site. Common tasks you'll perform include the following:

- ➤ Cropping and resizing an image
- ➤ Optimizing the file size of an image
- ➤ Overlaying anti-aliased text on an image
- ➤ Slicing up a large image into a set of smaller ones
- ➤ Adjusting an image's brightness, sharpness, or color
- ➤ Transforming an image through special filters

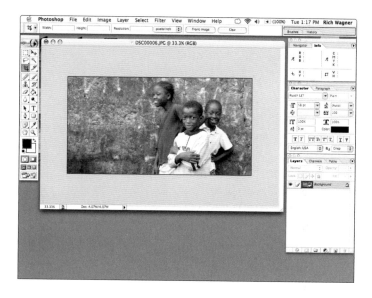

Web Browsers: Your Test Suite

Every Web designer has his favorite browser. Mainstreamers opt for *the* standard, the latest version of Microsoft Internet Explorer for Windows. Underdogs, on the other hand, root for Firefox, the "Young Turk" of the browser world. Mac fans love Safari, while others — particularly nonconformists or purists — opt for one of the many niche browsers available.

The problem comes in when you begin to unconsciously design a Web site specifically for your browser of choice, ignoring the idiosyncrasies and differences that exist with the others. For example, the figures on the right show the same HTML file in two browsers. Safari displays the Web page as intended, while Internet Explorer for Mac doesn't correctly display the menu or header.

Therefore, you want to be sure to test your made-over Web site on multiple browsers before going live. The more browsers you test on, the better. But, if you choose only two, be sure to choose Internet Explorer (80–85% market share) and Firefox (10%).

Rich's Take: If you use Windows exclusively and don't have access to a Mac, you can still perform a sanity check to ensure that your Web site displays properly with Mac's Safari browser. Go to www.danvine.com/icapture to use the free iCapture service. iCapture looks at the URL you submit and creates a JPG image of the Web page based on how the Web page displays in Safari. You can then view or download the resulting image.

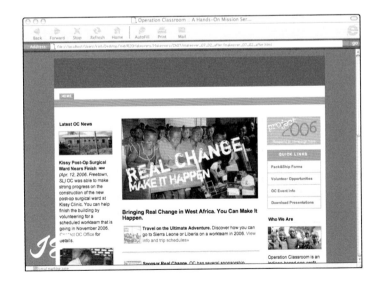

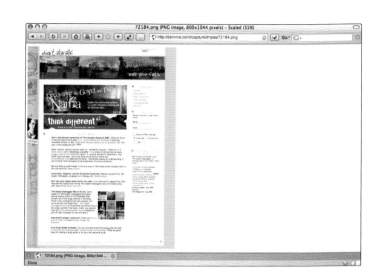

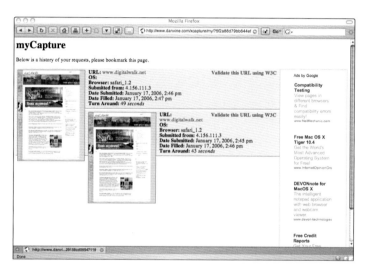

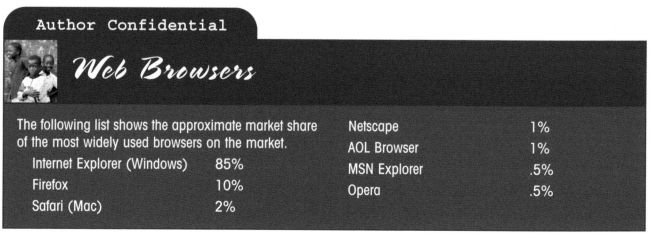

Web Developer Extension for Firefox: Your Interactive Debugging Environment

For much of the lifespan of the Web, debugging Web pages has been a trial-and-error process. It usually goes something like this: You do your best to design and code your page and then open it in your browser to test it. If something displays or executes incorrectly, then you redo the process.

However, a third-party extension available for the Firefox browser provides a "makeover of sorts" to the debugging process. The Web Developer extension is the handiest interactive debugging tool I've come across that takes much of the guesswork out of debugging.

For example, trying to debug CSS styles can be a painful and laborious process because of the cascading effects of the technology. Web Developer allows you to work with and modify CSS styles within the "live" browser environment itself.

Second, trying to understand the layout of a Web page can be confusing when working with multiple `div` elements or tables. The Web Developer extension allows you to easily label your block elements and provide outlines for these regions on your page.

Third, the Web Developer extension provides one-click access to several online analysis tools. You can view a speed report of your page, validate a page's HTML, links, CSS, and more.

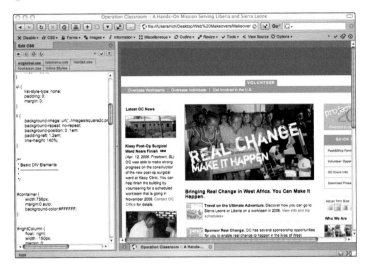

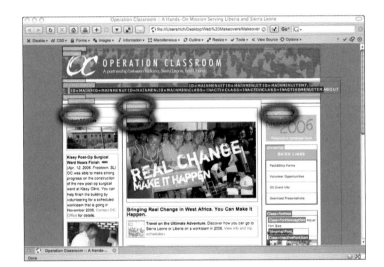

These examples are just a small sampling of the many features and capabilities of the Web Developer extension.

You can download the Web Developer extension at http://chrispederick.com/work/webdeveloper. The extension is made available under the terms of the GNU General Public License.

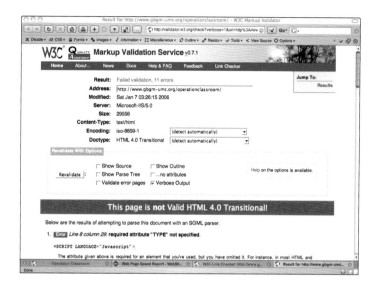

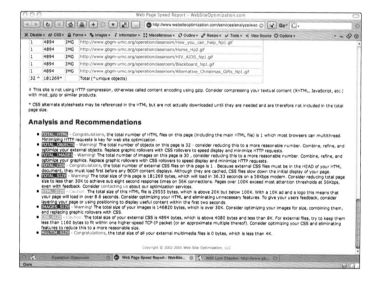

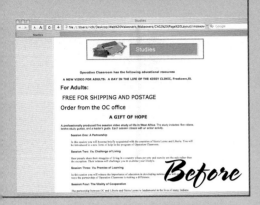

Before

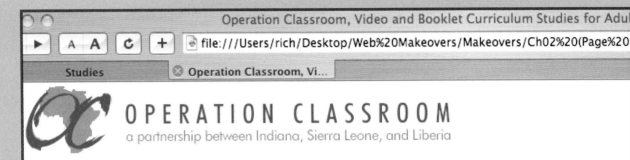

Studies

Operation Classroom has adult and children educational resources available for you.

Adults

A Gift of Hope

"A Gift of Hope" is a professionally produced five session video study of life in West Africa. The study includes: five videos, twelve st[u] and a leader's guide. Each session closes with an action activity.

Session One: A Partnership

In this session you will become briefly acquainted with the countries of Sierra Leone and Liberia. You will be introduced to a new form in the program of Operation Classroom.

Session Two: The Challenge of Living

Hear people share their struggles of living in a country where poverty and scarcity are the rule rather than the exception. Their witnes[s] challenge you to examine your lifestyle.

Session Three: The Promise of Learning

In this session you will witness the importance of education in developing nations. You will see some of the ways the partnership of O[peration] Classroom is making a difference.

Session Four: The Vitality of Cooperation

The church in Liberia and Sierra Leone is fundamental in the lives of many United Methodists. In this fourth video, you will experience of their joy as they bear witness to their faith in Christ. You will be invited to examine the vitality of your local church as well as of your personal faith.

Session Five: A Gift of Hope

United Methodists in West Africa share an unshakable hope, as they live in a country where poverty is routine. In this final session, th[e] African Christians will share with you their gift of hope.

The lesson format is patterned after the Disciple Bible Study format and is action-oriented.

The sale price for the 5 videos, 12 student manuals, and leader's guide is $19.95 plus $5.00 shipping and handling charge. Additional

After

2

PAGE LAYOUT MAKEOVERS

Where do I begin? That's the question you have to answer before you can start any project, whether it's for your home, garage, or Web site. Obviously, you want to begin by focusing your efforts on the base or bottom level and then work your way up from there. If, for example, you are doubling the size of your living room, you wouldn't want to begin by hanging new pictures. Instead, you'd knock out the unwanted wall, perform the necessary plaster work, paint the walls, and then consider which pictures to hang. In the same way, while I focus on many visual makeovers for your Web site in this book, you will want to make sure that your foundation — the page layout itself — is constructed to handle the makeovers you perform throughout the rest of the book.

In this chapter, you explore five makeovers that deal with the layout of your Web page. I begin by swapping out a table-based HTML page structure in favor of `div` elements, which offers a structure that is far easier and more efficient to work with. I then explore how to box in your page's content to give it the focus it needs, followed by a standardized way to offset the page header from the rest of your text. Next, you do a mini-makeover that centers your content in a user's browser, regardless of the browser's width. Finally, although HTML `div` elements are rectangular, I "round out" the chapter by showing you a nifty trick in Photoshop that makes your border corners look, well, rounded.

You can follow along in the chapter by applying the makeovers to your own Web pages. However, you can also feel free to work with the HTML files and images that I highlight in this chapter's makeovers. Each of the files and images that I use as examples in this chapter is available for download from the book's Web site.

Note: In this chapter, each of the makeovers builds upon the previous ones. Therefore, I recommend working through this chapter in sequence to achieve optimal results.

Moving from Table Layout to DIVs

Until recently, whether you created a Web page by hand or through a visual Web page builder, chances are you used tables to lay out your Web page. For much of the Web's history, HTML tables were a useful way to precisely position a page's layout. The problem is that table-based layouts are kludgy: Tables were meant to display spreadsheet-like data, not to be used as the primary building block for Web design. (Not sure what is meant by kludgy? Check out the Web site to the right.) Although you can get the visual results you want with tables, they are hard to work with and are difficult to tweak.

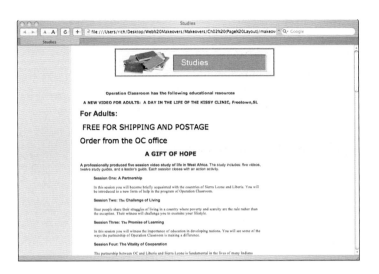

In recent years, the `div` element was introduced into HTML as a new block formatting element. Fortunately, the `div` element is now supported by all the major browsers and is the preferred way to lay out your Web design. Much like a table cell, the `div` element defines a rectangular block of your document. However, a `div` gives you far more control over where you place and format it.

Here's how to convert the table-based layout of a page into one that uses `div` elements and Cascading Stylesheets (CSS) to position the `div` elements.

❶ Start out with a new, basic HTML page.

Because you're going to throw away all of the table-based layout code, it's much easier to start with a fresh, clean HTML document. You can then copy and paste the text in from the old document after your layout is configured.

If you're using Dreamweaver, choose File⇨New and then select HTML from the Basic Page pane. Click the Create button to create the new document.

❷ Save the page.

The newly created page is automatically named `Untitled-1`. Before continuing, it is a good idea to save the file with a real file-name. Choose File⇨Save and have at it.

If you're working through the examples, save it under the name `makeover_02_01.html`.

❸ Create a basic CSS page.

You'll define the `div` elements and their content inside of the HTML page, but you'll use an external stylesheet to define the positioning and formatting of the `div` elements.

In Dreamweaver, once again choose File⇨New and then select CSS from the Basic Page pane. Click the Create button to create the new stylesheet.

❹ Save the stylesheet.

Choose File⇨Save and save the stylesheet. I recommend placing it in a subfolder named `css` underneath the base HTML directory.

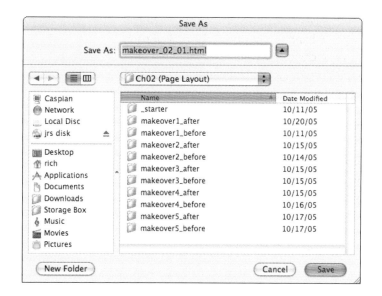

Author Confidential

External Stylesheets

Although you can embed CSS instructions inside your HTML page header, it's a good practice to keep your CSS code separate from your HTML page. Not only does this enable you to easily reuse the same CSS stylesheet for other pages on your site, but it also lets you modify your pages' formatting without even touching the Web page itself. Suppose, for example, that you wish to tweak the default typeface across your Web site. Without a centralized way to update this setting, you'd have to open up each of the pages on your site to make the change. However, with an external CSS stylesheet referenced by each of your pages, you need to make only one tweak to update the formatting of your entire Web site.

Moving from Table Layout to DIVs *(continued)*

If you're following this example to the letter, save it as `makeover_02_01.css`.

❺ Activate the HTML Page window and go into Code view.

In Dreamweaver, click the HTML page's tab and then click the Code button on the Document toolbar.

If you use Dreamweaver, you'll notice that basic document meta data is already added at the top of the page.

When you're inside the code itself, you are ready to set up the `div` elements inside your Web page. For those of you wanting a score card, you use the `header div` to display a logo graphic, and the `container div` serves as a wrapper containing all of the page's content. Inside of `container`, the `content div` contains the main page's content, while the `rightColumn div` is a column for sidebar elements. A `footer div` is added to the bottom of the page.

❻ Type the `div` element code into the document body.

Enter `div` elements for each of the sections of the document, identifying them with `id` attributes, as shown here to the right. These unique identifiers will be used for customizing the formatting for each of these block elements.

You'll come back and add content to the `content` and `rightColumn div` elements later, but first you need to set up the stylesheet.

Before leaving the HTML page, link the CSS stylesheet you'll be working with by adding the following code to the document head:

```
<link rel="stylesheet"
rev="stylesheet"
href="css/makeover_02_01.css"
type="text/css" media="screen"
charset="utf-8" />
```

❼ Activate the CSS Page window.

In Dreamweaver, click the CSS page's tab.

You use the CSS stylesheet to specify the shape, size, and other formatting instructions for the individual `div` elements.

❽ Enter id selectors for each of the `div` elements.

An `id` selector contains a # symbol followed by the `id` value of the `div`. It is used to specify the formatting for elements with the associated `id`. Enter the selectors based on the example shown to the right.

In my example, the `header` element has a fixed height of 80px, a 20px left margin, and 90% width.

The `container` element expands to 90% of the browser window, but always has a 20px left margin.

The `content` element adds padding around its content and specifies a right margin of 175px, which will be taken up by the `rightColumn` element.

The `rightColumn` element sets the `float` style to `float:right`. This style specifies which side the `div` element is aligned to so that other content wraps around it. The `width` style is set to 150px, enabling it to fit comfortably within the margin set by the `content div`. Other margin and padding styles are also set.

A basic `footer` element is also defined here. I talk more about the `footer` element in Chapter 3.

Using a handy feature found in the Web Developer extension of Firefox, the figure on the right shows the outline of these empty `div` elements based on these CSS settings.

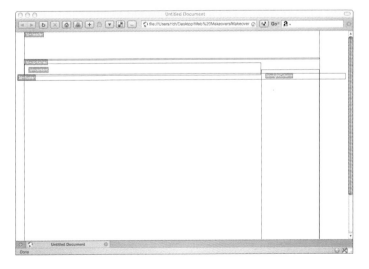

```css
 6
 7   #header {
 8       height : 80px;
 9       margin-left: 20px;
10       width:90%;
11   }
12
13   #container {
14       width:90%;
15       margin-left: 20px;
16   }
17
18   #content {
19       padding: 1em;
20       margin-right: 175px;
21   }
22
23   #rightColumn {
24       float : right;
25       width : 150px;
26       margin: 0;
27       margin-top: 20px;
28       padding: 1em;
29       min-height: 600px;
30   }
31
32   #footer {
33       clear: both;
34       text-align: left;
35       margin: 0px auto;
36       margin-top:0px;
37       width: 736px;
38       height: 40px;
39       line-height: 1.0em;
40       background-color:#FFFFFF;
41       padding: 1em 0 ;
42       padding-left: 10px;
43       padding-right: 10px;
44   }
45   |
46
47
48
```

1K / 1 sec

Moving from Table Layout to DIVs *(continued)*

Note: In this makeover, the layout stretches and contracts based on the size of the browser window. In the next makeover, you explore a fixed-width layout.

❾ Add general HTML styles.

Although the focus of this makeover is on the layout, take a moment to add two general HTML styles for the `body` and `p` elements. The `margin-top` rule for the `body` sets the top margin to 0 pixels, while the other two rules set basic text formatting. I talk more about text makeovers in Chapter 5.

❿ Still in the CSS page, add id selectors for those `p` and `h2` elements that appear in your `rightColumn div`.

Add these id selectors after the `footer` id selector, which you added in Step 8.

For the `p` elements, specify the top and bottom margins. For `h2` elements, define the font, margin, and bottom border to help offset an `h2` caption title from the normal text.

⓫ Choose File➪Save to save changes to the CSS page.

Get in the habit of saving early and often.

Now that your CSS styles are defined, you are ready to add the Web page's content to your newly created HTML page.

To save time on the chore of typing, lift whatever text you can from your original Web page. To that end, you'll want to open the original page in your browser of choice.

⓬ Open your original Web page in your browser.

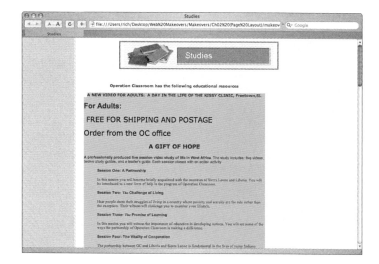

⑬ Copy the text you wish to use as your new page's main content.

Select the text in your browser and then choose Edit⇨Copy.

⑭ Paste the text inside the `content div` element.

In Dreamweaver, activate the HTML page's editing window, place the text cursor just after the `<div id="content">` tag, and then choose Edit⇨Paste.

⑮ Repeat Steps 13 and 14 for any text you wish to place in the `rightColumn div`.

The right-hand sidebar column is often used for special notices or additional navigation options.

⑯ Add your logo or other banner image inside your `header div`.

Position your text cursor just after the `<div id="header">` tag. Enter an `<img>` element referencing the desired graphic to display in the header. Or, in Dreamweaver, choose Insert⇨Image and select the image from the Select Image Source dialog box.

⑰ Edit and format your document text as desired.

Before finishing the makeover, you may wish to edit and format the page's text.

⑱ Save changes to your HTML page.

After you complete these steps, the content of your Web page is surprisingly ready to go. (In Dreamweaver, you just choose File⇨Save to save your changes.)

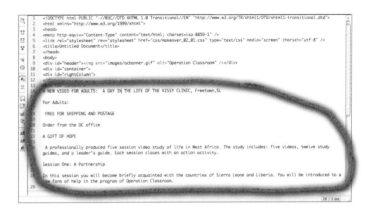

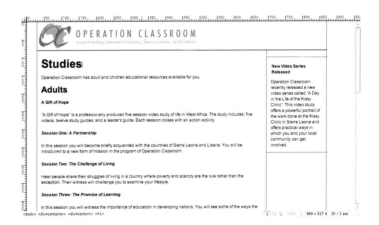

Moving from Table Layout to DIVs (continued)

⑲ View your new layout in your browser.

Take a look at your new page layout in your default browser. (In Dreamweaver, for example, pressing F12 takes you right there.)

Note: In addition to the changes discussed in the makeover, you'll notice the banner graphic and background are different as well. While the end result to this makeover looks somewhat plain, the makeovers that follow help enhance what you started here.

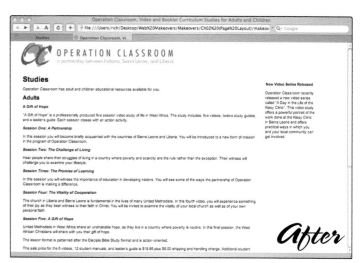

Author Confidential

Liquid vs. Fixed Layouts

Layouts that adjust their sizes automatically based on the dimensions of the browser window are often called *liquid layouts. Fixed layouts,* on the other hand, have a permanent size, regardless of the size of the browser window itself or the video resolution of the computer. Liquid layouts are flexible; they make effective use of all of the real estate in the browser window. In contrast, fixed layouts give you precise control over how the page is presented in all circumstances. Liquid layouts work ideally for sites like Amazon.com that have so much content that they need to use every pixel of the screen they can. However, fixed layouts can be the best choice if you want to have greater control over the site's look and overall user experience.

Boxing in Your Page's Content

When you frame an 8 x 10 photograph, you often overlay the picture with a *matte*. A matte is used to complement the picture and to naturally steer the eye toward the photo itself.

You can achieve a similar result on your Web site by adding a border around your page's content and then giving your Web page's background a color that complements your overall design.

You can perform this makeover on a page that expands and contracts based on the size of the browser. However, for greater control, you'll want to fix the size of your content's area to a width under 800 pixels. I recommend 756 pixels.

Note: This makeover assumes you are using `div` elements to enclose your page's content and CSS to format these elements. Therefore, be sure you work through the first makeover in this chapter before you continue.

Here's how to perform this makeover. (You can see an example of a page in need of a virtual "matte" here to the right.)

❶ Open the CSS stylesheet that contains the HTML page's formatting instructions.

If you are using the book's example files, open the `makeover_02_02.css` file.

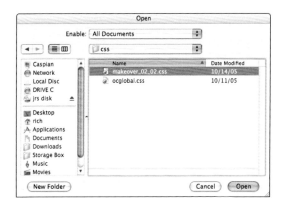

❷ Add a background color to the `body` selector.

Locate the `body` selector in the CSS stylesheet and add a `background-color` style and a valid color specification.

For the book example, specify the following background color:

```
background-color: #697172;
```

Boxing in Your Page's Content *(continued)*

In your project, choose a color that complements your overall color scheme without drawing attention to itself. For most purposes, you'll want to choose a dark, non-bright color.

❸ Specify the exact width for the `container div` element.

Locate the `#container` selector in the CSS stylesheet. Change the width from `90%` to a pixel-based size:

```
width:756px;
```

Regardless of the size of the browser window, the page's content will now be enclosed within the fixed width of the `container div`.

❹ Specify a white background for the `container div` element.

By default, `div` elements have a transparent background. In order to offset the `container div`'s content from the background color of the page, you need to specify a background color for the `container div` as well.

In order to maximize readability, a white or off-white background is often the best color to use as the background for your content. For the book example, I chose white, which is specified with the following style:

```
background-color: #FFFFFF;
```

❺ Change the size of the `header div` element.

Locate the `#header` selector in the CSS stylesheet. Just like `container`, change its width to a pixel-based size:

```
width:756px;
```

❻ Add a background color to the `header div` element.

The header also needs to have a distinct color to separate it from the page's

```
/**
 * General HTML Body Styling
 * -----------------------------
 */
body {
          ...ca, sans-serif;
    background-color: #69717...
}

p { line-height: 1.95em; }

h1 {
    font: 185%/1em Arial, Helvetica, sans-serif;
    font-size: 1.95em;
    font-weight: bold;
}

/**
 * Basic DIV Elements
 * -----------------------------
 *
 */

#container {
    width:756px;
```

```
/**
 * Basic DIV Elements
 * -----------------------------
 *
 */

#container {
    width:756px;
    margin-left: 10px;
    background-color:#FFFFFF;
}
```

background. You may wish to have it the same color as your container. Or, as in the book's example, you may want to offset it as a different color.

Enter a color style in the #header selector:

```
background-color:#1D6963;
```

❼ Save changes to your CSS stylesheet.

Choose File⇨Save to save your changes. Because all of your formatting is done through CSS, you don't have to alter the content of the HTML page at all.

❽ View your new page look in your browser.

Open your HTML page in your browser to view the results of the makeover. If you are following along with the book's examples, open makeover_02_02.html.

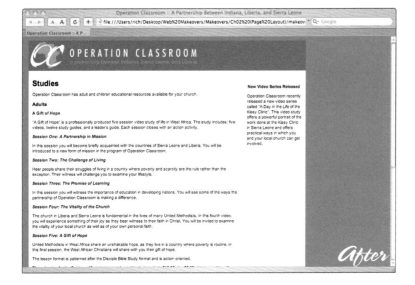

Adding a Page Heading

For many Web page layouts, an important component is a heading that identifies the content of your page. h1 elements are often used, but I show you a makeover that allows for even greater flexibility by using div elements.

On occasion, you may wish to embed text inside of a graphic for a more eye-grabbing page header. Chapter 4, in fact, shows just such an example. However, ordinary text is usually the best option. It's more accessible and easier to manage.

Check out the steps for this makeover.

① Open an HTML page that you wish to add a page header to.

Choose File➪Open in Dreamweaver.

If you're working through the examples I've come up with, open makeover_02_03.html.

② View the HTML code for the page.

In Dreamweaver, click the Code button on the Document toolbar.

③ Scroll down to the content div element.

In the basic five-div layout structure, you'll find it easiest to place the header inside the content div.

④ Locate the existing page heading and enclose the text with the necessary tags for a div element.

Using a div element enables you to set up an id selector that is customized for just the page heading, rather than targeting all h1 elements on a page.

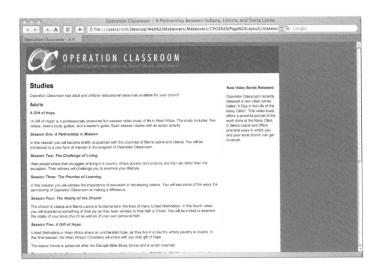

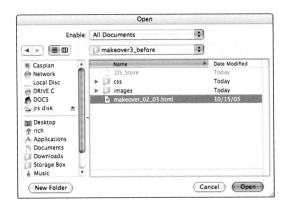

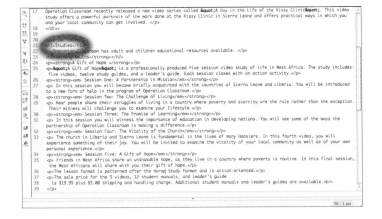

Replace any tags that you may have around your heading text with this (where *Heading* is your text):

```
<div
id="pageheading">Heading</div>
```

❺ Add a new headingspacer div element.

Below the page heading, add a new div element called headingspacer. You'll define a spacing graphic that helps offset the heading from the rest of the page. Here's the code:

```
<div id="headingspacer"></div>
```

❻ Choose File⇨Save to save changes to your HTML page.

No sense taking chances on losing all that work, right?

❼ Open your CSS stylesheet.

Once again, choose File⇨Open and use the dialog box to open up the stylesheet you are using that defines your site design.

For the book's example, locate and open the makeover_02_03.css file (you know, the one with header, container, content, rightColumn, and footer).

❽ Add an id selector for the pageheading div.

You usually want the page heading text to be noticeably larger than your normal text — larger than any other headings that you may have, as a matter of fact. To do that, you should define your page heading as being 3.25em in size, with a font-weight of bold. (I'd also add padding to the top and bottom of the div.)

For the book example, I colored the text dark gray (#999999) as a complementary color to the main color scheme.

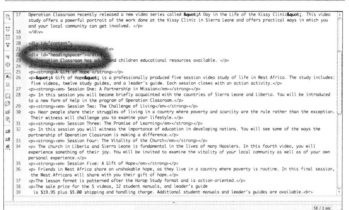

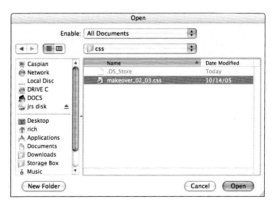

Adding a Page Heading *(continued)*

⑨ Add an id selector for the `headingspacer` **div.**

The `headingspacer div` displays a horizontal line graphic below the page heading. Using a graphic here helps visually offset the page heading from the rest of the page.

The `background-image`, with `background-repeat:no-repeat;`, is a great way to place an image into your `div` element without directly adding it into your HTML code.

You can use any graphic you like, but make its dimensions 581 x 22 pixels.

The book example uses `pagetitle spacer.gif`, located in the Images subfolder.

Enter the selector code as shown to the right.

⑩ When you have finished entering both selectors, choose File⇨ Save.

Doing so saves the CSS stylesheet.

⑪ View your new page heading in your browser.

Activate your HTML file in Dreamweaver by clicking its document tab. Then, press F12 to display the page heading in your default browser.

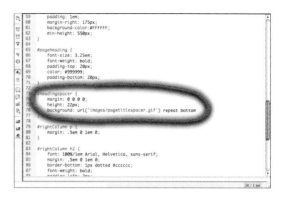

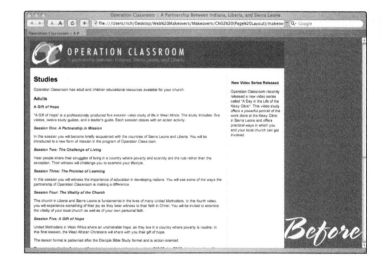

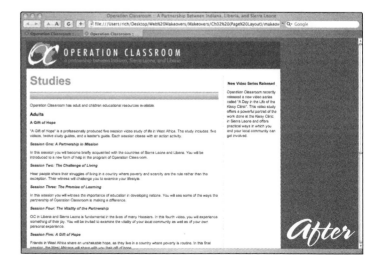

Centering Your Pages

If everyone had the same browser size and screen resolution, you could align your page layout to the center of the screen simply by positioning it at the appropriate pixel position. However, because the resolution could be as small as 800 x 600 (on some older systems) to as large as 1280 x 1024 or higher, you never know exactly the correct screen coordinates beforehand. In the earlier makeovers, I use a 10px left margin. But a left-aligned page usually doesn't look as nice as a center-aligned one. (Check out the Web page to the right to see what I mean.)

Here's a makeover that tweaks a couple styles in your stylesheet to center your pages.

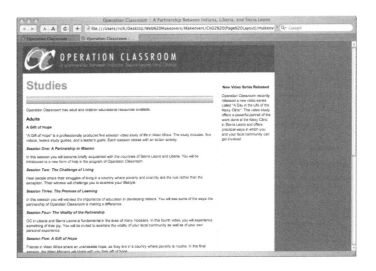

❶ Open the CSS stylesheet that contains your HTML page's formatting instructions.

If you're using the book's example files, open the `makeover_02_04.css` file.

❷ Change the margin style of the `#header` selector.

Locate the `#header` selector in your CSS stylesheet and then change the margin to

```
margin: 0 auto;
```

This declaration sets the horizontal alignment to the center.

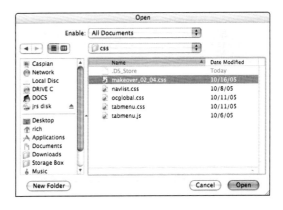

❸ Add a text-align style to the `#header` selector.

Add this code:

```
text-align: center;
```

Although the margin style normally handles the centering, there is a special case you need to account for. If Internet Explorer operates in what is called *quirks mode,* the Microsoft browser won't render this as you expect. Therefore, to safeguard against that, you'll want to add two more steps.

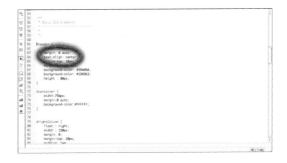

Centering Your Pages *(continued)*

④ Repeat steps 2 and 3 for the #container selector.

You want to be sure all of your primary div elements are centered in the browser.

⑤ Add a text-align style to the #content and rightColumn selectors.

In order to ensure that your text-align workaround for Internet Explorer's quirks mode doesn't impact your other content, add the following line to your #content and #rightColumn selectors:

```
text-align: left;
```

⑥ Save your CSS stylesheet.

After you've finished adding these styles, choose File➪Save to save your changes.

⑦ View your new page look in your browser.

Open your HTML page in your browser to view the results of the makeover. If you are following along with the book's examples, open makeover_01_04.html.

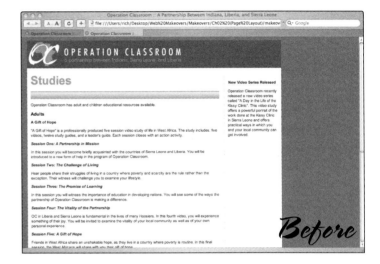

Before

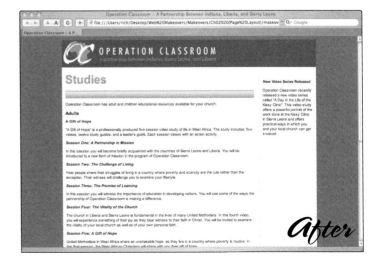

After

Adding Curves to Your Edges

When you design for the Web, you normally assemble a set of rectangular blocks — either `div` or `table` elements — in a certain manner to achieve the look you're after. While the "rectangular blocks" approach (see the page to the right) is great for creating sharp-looking square edges, the "sharp look" may not necessarily be what you're after. One makeover you can perform to your pages is to round the corners of your page borders. Rounded corners add a subtle touch of style and help "round out" your page layout design.

Unfortunately, nothing in the block-based worlds of HTML and CSS can give you rounded corners. You have to create them on your own in Photoshop (or another graphics editor) and then seamlessly add them into your page layout.

Here's how to perform this makeover:

❶ In Photoshop, choose File⇨New and create a new document.

Go for one with dimensions of 758 x 8 pixels, a resolution of 72 pixels per inch, and sporting a transparent background.

Using a transparent background enables you to use rounded corners no matter what the background color of your page is.

❷ Create a new layer by choosing Layer⇨New⇨Layer.

Name the layer `Border` in the New Layer dialog box and then click OK.

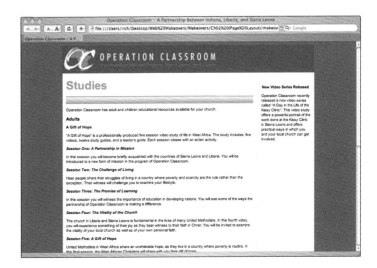

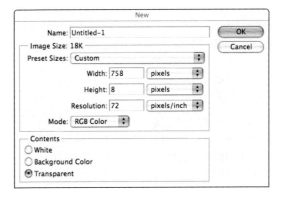

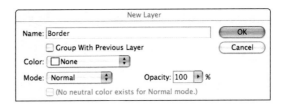

Adding Curves to Your Edges *(continued)*

③ Double-click the Foreground Color box in the Tools palette.

The Color Picker dialog box makes an appearance.

You want to match the color of your border to that of your `header div` background color so that your rounded border blends in perfectly with the header.

If you are following along with the book example, enter 59A09A in the hex color box provided and then click OK to close out the Color Picker.

④ Choose the Rounded Rectangle tool from the Tools palette.

Doing so calls up the Options bar for the tool.

⑤ In the Options bar, enter the amount of curve you want in the Radius field.

The Radius property sets the amount of curve used in the rounded corners. Use 10px to achieve the intended look.

⑥ Enlarge the document window as needed to display the gray area outside the canvas.

You need to be able to see space beyond the canvas when you size the rounded rectangle.

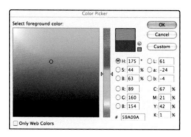

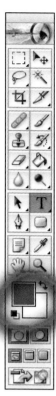

⑦ Draw a rounded rectangle with dimensions of 756 x 43px.

Click the down arrow on the Options bar to display the Rounded Rectangle Options box. Click the Fixed Sized option and then enter 756 in the W box and 43 in the H box.

Starting near the top-left side of the canvas, draw the fixed-size rounded rectangle. Obviously, most of the height of the rectangle will extend below the canvas.

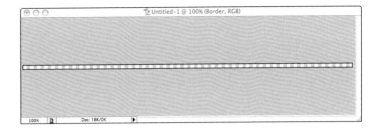

⑧ Align the top of the rectangle with the top of the canvas.

The rectangle shape should have a Y coordinate of 0.

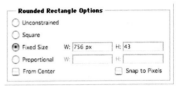

⑨ Reposition the rectangle to have a 1px margin on the left and right.

The shape should have an X coordinate of 1.

⑩ Save your working file.

You export the graphic as a GIF file for use on your Web site in the next step, but be sure to first save your working file.

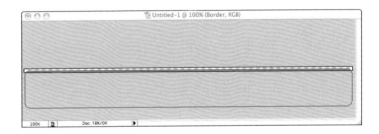

Choose File⇨Save and name the file topborder.psd or another descriptive filename.

⑪ Save as a GIF file for use on your Web site.

Choose File⇨Save for Web from the Photoshop menu.

Adding Curves to Your Edges *(continued)*

Select GIF from the Optimized File Format drop-down list. *Note:* Because of the transparent background, be sure to save the image either in GIF or PNG format. JPG images do not support transparency.

Check the Transparency checkbox if it is not selected already.

⑫ Click the Save button in the Save for Web dialog box.

The Save Optimized As dialog box makes an appearance.

⑬ Save your top border image.

Navigate to your Images directory for your Web site, enter topborder.gif in the File Name box, and click Save.

Your top border is now ready. You now need to create a rounded border for the bottom of the page.

⑭ Choose Image⇨Duplicate from the menu.

You use the image copy to create the bottom border.

⑮ Choose Image⇨Rotate Canvas⇨Flip Canvas Vertical.

This command flips the image upside down, exactly as you want the bottom border to look.

You now need to color the border to match the background color of your footer div. If the color is identical to your top border, then you can skip Step 15. Otherwise proceed.

If you are working through the book's example, you need to perform Steps 16 and 17.

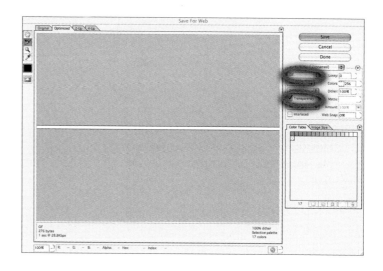

⑯ Double-click the Border layer's thumbnail in the Layers palette.

The Color Picker is displayed.

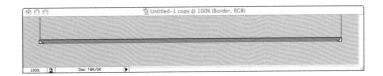

⑰ Select the correct color for the bottom border.

If you are following along with the book example, enter FFFFFF in the hex color box provided.

Click OK to close out the Color Picker.

⑱ Save a working file (in Photoshop format) for your bottom border file.

Choose File⇨Save As and name the file botborder.psd or another descriptive filename.

⑲ Save as a GIF file for use on your Web site.

Choose File⇨Save for Web from the Photoshop menu.

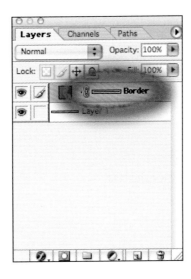

Once again, select GIF from the Optimized File Format drop-down menu.

Check the Transparency checkbox if it is not selected already.

⑳ Click the Save button in the Save for Web dialog box.

The Save Optimized As dialog box is displayed.

㉑ Save the file.

Navigate to your Images directory for your Web site and enter botborder.gif in the File Name box.

Your bottom border is now ready.

You're now ready to add the rounded border images to your Web page.

Adding Curves to Your Edges *(continued)*

㉒ Open an HTML page in which you wish to add rounded corners to the page border.

In Dreamweaver, you choose File⇨Open.

If you are working through the book examples, open `makeover_02_05.html`.

㉓ View the HTML code for the page.

In Dreamweaver, click the Code button on the Document toolbar.

㉔ Add a new `div` element called `topBorder` before the header div.

Locate the `header` div in your HTML page (just after the opening `<body>` tag). Add the following code before it:

```
<div id="topBorder"></div>
```

This `div` element will house the upper rounded corners.

㉕ Add a new `div` element called `bottomBorder` after the footer element.

Locate the `footer` div and add the following line of code after it:

```
<div id="bottomBorder"></div>
```

This `div` contains the lower rounded corners.

㉖ Open the CSS stylesheet that contains the HTML page's formatting instructions.

You need to specify the top and bottom border graphics as backgrounds for the `div` elements you just defined.

If you're using the book's example files, open the `makeover_02_05.css` file.

㉗ Add id selectors for the `topBorder` and `bottomBorder` div elements.

In the stylesheet, add `#topBorder` and `#bottomBorder` selectors by typing the code exactly as it appears in the figure to the right.

These selectors define the margin, dimensions, and background image for your borders.

㉘ Choose File➪Save to save your stylesheet.

It's no good to you if you don't save it.

㉙ View your new page look in your browser.

Open the HTML page in your browser to view the final results of the makeover. If you are following along with the book's examples, open `makeover_02_05.html`.

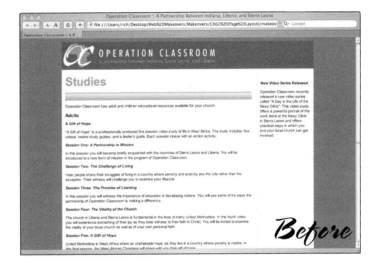

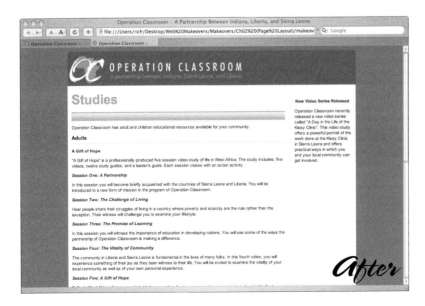

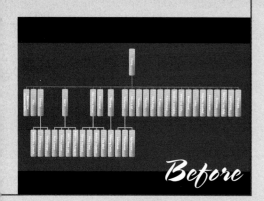

Before

After

3

NAVIGATION MAKEOVERS

A well-organized Web site is much like a GPS for your car: It lays out an appropriate amount of information based on your context to help you navigate to your desired destination. A GPS never attempts to overload you with directions coming up 100 miles down the road. Instead, it focuses on where you are at a specific geographic point. Similarly, in order for visitors to effectively navigate your Web site, you need to make it easy for them to find the information they need without overloading them with too many choices.

Unfortunately, many Web sites are about as easy to navigate as Boston with your eyes closed. Sometimes the problem is poor organization; other times it's a confusing menu system. Still other sites have no visual way of communicating exactly where you are on the site itself.

In this chapter, you explore five makeovers that will make your Web site easier for your visitors to navigate. You begin by reorganizing an existing Web site into one that flows much more logically. You then roll that hierarchy into a CSS-based, multi-level top menu system. Next, you explore a sidebar navigation makeover that transforms a simple bulleted list into something far more eye-appealing. Even if you have a well-organized site and easy-to-use menu, visitors can still lose their place in your site. The next makeover explores a simple technique that puts each page in its proper context. Finally, I show you how you can add a drop-down combo box list of your favorite site links.

Reorganizing Your Site for Easier Navigation

Some Web sites have a natural hierarchy to them, with their pages effortlessly falling into place. Others, however, take a bit of "elbow grease" to mold into a structure that makes sense for visitors navigating the site.

Here's a makeover in which you reorganize your Web site and transform it into a structure that your visitors don't need to be Magellans to navigate.

For the book example, I reorganize the Web site of a nonprofit organization known as Operation Classroom. (The Web site's Can't-See-the-Forest-for-the-Trees look is captured in the schematic diagram to the right.) Feel free to follow along with this example.

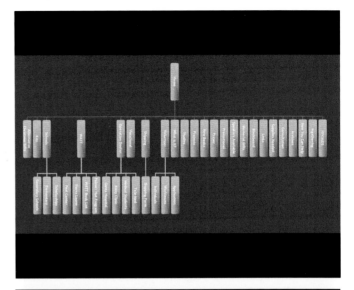

❶ On paper or on your computer, list all of your Web pages.

Forget whatever existing structure you have in place. Simply write out each page in a flat list. You can leave out the home page because that is the obvious first level in your hierarchy.

❷ Arrange pages in natural topic-oriented clusters.

Your pages usually fall into broader topics. Think about each page from a visitor's perspective and begin to arrange them accordingly.

In the book example, the pages fall into four clusters: about the organization, description of programs, getting involved, and resources available.

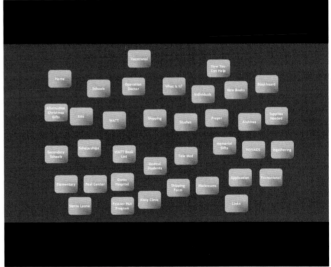

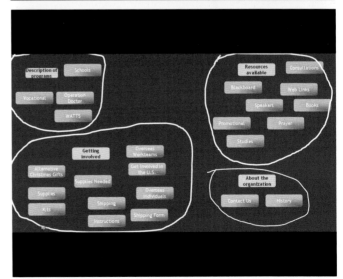

❸ Give each cluster a "down-to-earth" name in which its contents can be easily understood.

One potential downside to hierarchies is that you can come up with categories of pages that are too general, abstract, or vague. Therefore, make sure that visitors coming to your site can intuitively understand the labels you use for these clusters.

These category names will be the second-level headings in your navigation menu on your Web site.

Note: Don't get cute when naming the sections of your pages. For example, if your company sells products and services, label the associated page clusters "products" and "services" rather than terms that can be confusing for people unfamiliar with your company's offerings.

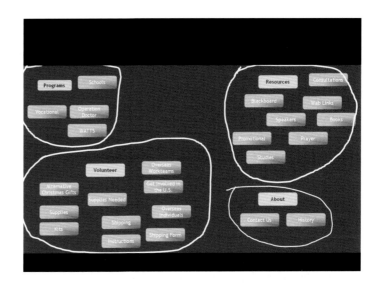

❹ Within the clusters, look for possible sub-clusters.

If you have similar topics that fit into a sub-category, arrange these together and label the sub-cluster based on the issues discussed in Step 3.

Note: Aim to keep your Web site to 2 or 3 heading levels under the home page if at all possible. Studies show that visitors get lost when they have to dive any deeper into a site's hierarchy than three levels.

❺ Re-examine your clusters to see whether any pages should be linked directly from the home page, even if it doesn't make perfect sense from a hierarchical perspective.

Although Web sites usually work best when you have an organized hierarchy, don't let neatness and order become a burden to the site's effectiveness. Check to see whether any topics inside your categories are important enough to your visitors to warrant separating out and adding as separate first-level categories.

In the book example, the Operation Classroom Web site had a topic (Shipping) that, purely from a hierarchical perspective, fell into the Getting Involved category. However, because many people visit the existing Web site specifically for information on shipping, I raised that topic to a first-level category and tweaked the "Getting Involved" label to something more appropriate for the remaining pages (Volunteer).

❻ Restructure your Web site with your new hierarchy.

After you finish this organizational exercise, you're ready to begin the task of structuring your site, which is discussed in the next makeover.

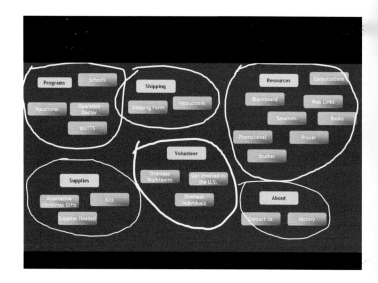

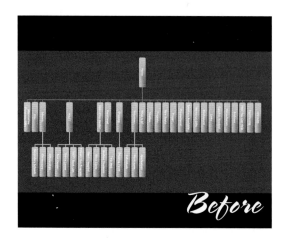

Before

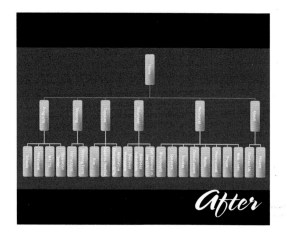

After

Creating a Top-Level Menu Bar

The structure of a Web site is shown to the visitor through your navigation. By and large, the most popular form of navigation is a top-level horizontal menu.

Here's a makeover for quickly adding a two-tier menu bar to your Web site.

Download `menubar.css` and `menubar.js` from the book's Web site and copy them into your Web site's css subfolder. Follow these instructions to add the menu bar to your site.

❶ Open an HTML page to which you wish to add a top-level menu bar.

In Dreamweaver, you do that by choosing File➪Open.

If you're working with the book examples, open the `makeover_03_03.html` file.

❷ View the HTML code for the page.

In Dreamweaver, click the Code button on the Document toolbar.

❸ Add a `link` element in your document header connecting the `tabmenu.css` stylesheet with your HTML page.

Type the following code in your document header:

```
<link rel="stylesheet"
rev="stylesheet" href="css/tab-
menu.css" type="text/css"
media="screen" charset="utf-8"
/>
```

The `tabmenu.css` provides formatting instructions for your menu bar.

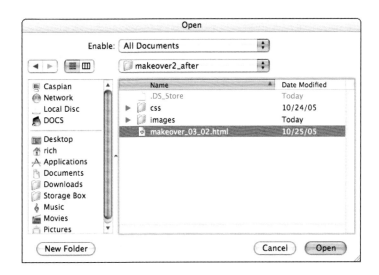

④ Add a script **element connecting** tabmenu.js **with your HTML page.**

Add the following HTML into the document header:

```
<script src="css/tabmenu.js"
type="text/javascript" lan-
guage="Javascript1.2"
charset="utf-8"></script>
```

The tabmenu.js code provides the interactivity for the menu bar.

⑤ Just inside the container div, **add a new** mainMenu div.

The mainmenu div displays all of the first-level items on your menu bar. Begin by adding the div element:

```
<div id="mainMenu">
</div>
```

⑥ Add an a **element inside the** mainMenu div **for each first-level menu item.**

Use the following code line as a model for your entries:

```
<a class="inactiveMenuItem"
style="left: 15px;"
id="mainMenuItem1"
href="index.html">Home</a>
```

The class attribute receives a value of either inactiveMenuItem or activeMenuItem. (Only one item should be initially set to active. This value is dependent on the context of the page you are working with.)

The style attribute assigns the left position for each entry. Begin with 15px and increment each successive a element by 85px.

Assign a unique identifier to the id attribute.

Add a URL to jump to in the href attribute in case the menu item is clicked.

```
1   <!DOCTYPE HTML PUBLIC "-//W3C//DTD HTML 4.01//EN" "http://www.w3.org/TR/html4/strict.dtd">
2   <html>
3   <head>
4   <title>Operation Classroom :: Indiana, Liberia and Sierra Leone</title>
5   <link rel="stylesheet" rev="stylesheet" href="css/tabmenu.css" type="text/css" media="screen" charset="utf-8" />
6   <script src="css/tabmenu.js" type="text/javascript" language="Javascript1.2" charset="utf-8"></script>
8   </head>
9
10  <body bgcolor="#697172">
11  <div id="topBorder"> </div>
12  <div id="header"></div
13  <div id="container">
14
15  <div id="rightColumn">
16  <h2>New Video Series Released </h2>
17  <p>
18  Operation Classroom recently released a new video series called &quot;A Day in the Life of the Kissy Clinic&quot;. This video
    study offers a powerful portrait of the work done at the Kissy Clinic in Sierra Leone and offers practical ways in which you and
    your local church can get involved. </p>
19  </div>
20
21  <div id="content">
22  <div id="pagetitle">Studies</div>
23  <div id="pagetitlespacer"></div>
24
25  <p>Operation Classroom has adult and children educational resources available for you. </p>
26  <h2><strong>Adults</strong></h2>
27  <p><strong>A Gift of Hope </strong></p>
28  <p>&quot;A Gift of Hope&quot; is a professionally produced five session video study of life in West Africa. The study includes:
    five videos, twelve study guides, and a leader's guide. Each session closes with an action activity.</p>
```

Finally, add a value for the a element — Programs, Shipping, Supplies, whatever — which serves as the visual text that appears for the menu item.

If you're working through the book example, enter the code as shown to the right.

❼ Just below the `mainMenu div`, add a subMenu div container to house all of the submenu items for each main menu item.

The `subMenu div` serves as a containing element for the submenu items. Type in the following code:

```
<div id="subMenu">
</div>
```

❽ Inside the `subMenu div` container, add a `div` for each of the submenu item groups.

All of the submenu items associated with a top-level menu item need to be grouped together in a `div` element. The name of the `div` is `submenu_` plus a sequential number (`submenu_1`, `submenu2`, . . .).

Here's the HTML code for the initial `div`:

```
<div style="padding-left: 15px;
position: static; display:
none;" id="submenu_1">
</div>
```

The `style` attribute defines the formatting used to display the `div`. Leave `display: none` for each element, except for the submenu item group that is associated with the `activeMenuItem` marked in Step 5.

Repeat for each submenu item cluster.

Note: Even if the top-level menu item doesn't contain any submenu items, you still need a submenu `div` associated with it.

Creating a Top-Level Menu Bar *(continued)*

⑨ Inside each of these div **elements, add an** a **element for each item in the submenu.**

The a elements inside the submenu are plain, ordinary a elements. Here's an example:

```
<div style="padding-left: 15px;
position: static; display:
none;" id="submenu_2">
<a href="programs/schools.html"
>Schools</a> |
<a href="programs/vocational.
html">Vocational</a> |
<a href="programs/training.
html/">WATTS</a> |
<a href="programs/medical.
html">Operation Doctor</a>
</div>
```

You'll notice that I add a vertical bar (|) between each a element. This optional symbol provides a visual separator between the submenu items.

If you're working with the example from the book, here's the entire submenu code:

```
<div id="submenu">
   <div style="padding-left:
15px; position: static; dis-
play: none;" id="submenu_1">
   </div>
   <div style="padding-left:
15px; position: static; dis-
play: none;" id="submenu_2">
      <a
href="../programs/schools.html">
Schools</a> |
      <a
href="../programs/vocational.htm
l">Vocational</a> |
```

```html
        <a
href="../programs/training.html"
>WATTS</a> |
        <a href="../programs/med-
ical.html">Operation Doctor</a>
    </div>
    <div style="padding-left:
15px; position: static; dis-
play: none;" id="submenu_3">
        <a
href="../shipping/howto.html">In
structions</a> |
        <a
href="../shipping/shipform.html"
>Shipping Form</a>
    </div>
    <div style="padding-left:
15px; position: static; dis-
play: none;" id="submenu_4">
        <a
href="../supplies/kits.html">Kit
s</a> |
        <a
href="../supplies/needs.html">Su
pplies Needed</a> |
        <a href="../supplies/alt-
gifts.html">Alternative
Christmas Gifts</a>
    </div>
    <div style="padding-left:
15px; position: static; dis-
play: none;" id="submenu_5">
        <a
href="../volunteer/workteams.htm
l">Overseas Workteams</a> |
        <a
href="../volunteer/indy.html">Ov
erseas Individuals</a> |
        <a
href="../supplies/domestic.html"
>Get Involved in the U.S.</a>
    </div>
```

Creating a Top-Level Menu Bar *(continued)*

```html
      <div style="padding-left:
15px; position: static; dis-
play: none;" id="submenu_6">
      <a
href="../resources/blackboard.ht
ml">Blackboard</a> |
      <a
href="../resources/speakers.html
/">Speakers</a> |
      <a
href="../resources/studies.html/
">Studies</a> |
      <a
href="../resources/consult.html/
">Consultations</a> |
      <a
href="../resources/books.html/">
Books</a> |
      <a
href="../resources/ocgear.html/"
>Promotional</a> |
      <a
href="../resources/prayer.html/"
>Prayer</a> |
      <a
href="../resources/links.html/">
Web Links</a>
    </div>
    <div style="padding-left:
15px; position: static; dis-
play: none;" id="submenu_7">
      <a href="../about/contac-
tus.html/">Contact Us</a> |
      <a href="../about/his-
tory.html/">History</a>
    </div>
</div>
```

⑩ Save your changes to the HTML page.

In Dreamweaver, choose File⇨Save from the main menu.

```html
23   <div id="submenu">
24
25      </div>
26      <div style="padding-left: 15px; position: static; display: none;" id="submenu_2">
27        <a href="../programs/schools.html">Schools</a> |
28        <a href="../programs/vocational.html">Vocational</a> |
29        <a href="../programs/training.html">MATTS</a> |
30        <a href="../programs/medical.html">Operation Doctor</a>
31
32      <div style="padding-left: 15px; position: static; display: none;" id="submenu_3">
33        <a href="../shipping/howto.html">Instructions</a> |
34        <a href="../shipping/shipform.html">Shipping Form</a>
35      </div>
36      <div style="padding-left: 15px; position: static; display: none;" id="submenu_4">
37        <a href="../supplies/kits.html">Kits</a> |
38        <a href="../supplies/needs.html">Supplies Needed</a> |
39        <a href="../supplies/altgifts.html">Alternative Christmas Gifts</a>
40      </div>
41      <div style="padding-left: 15px; position: static; display: none;" id="submenu_5">
42        <a href="../volunteer/workteams.html">Overseas Workteams</a> |
43        <a href="../volunteer/indy.html">Overseas Individuals</a> |
44        <a href="../supplies/domestic.html">Get Involved in the U.S.</a>
45      </div>
46      <div style="padding-left: 15px; position: static; display: none;" id="submenu_6">
47        <a href="../resources/blackboard.html">Blackboard</a> |
48        <a href="../resources/speakers.html/">Speakers</a> |
49        <a href="../resources/studies.html/">Studies</a> |
50        <a href="../resources/consult.html/">Consultations</a> |
51        <a href="../resources/books.html/">Books</a> |
52        <a href="../resources/ocgear.html/">Promotional</a> |
53        <a href="../resources/prayer.html/">Prayer</a> |
54        <a href="../resources/links.html/">Web Links</a>
55      </div>
56      <div style="padding-left: 15px; position: static; display: none;" id="submenu_7">
57        <a href="../about/contactus.html/">Contact Us</a> |
58        <a href="../about/history.html/">History</a>
59      </div>
60   </div>
61
```

`<head>`   5K / 1 sec

⑪ Open the `tabmenu.css` file.

Choose File⇨Open and select `tabmenu.css` to open for editing inside of Dreamweaver.

The `tabmenu.css` stylesheet sets the color and other formatting properties for your menu bar. You'll want to customize the colors to match your Web site color scheme.

If you're working through the book example, you don't need to make any changes to the stylesheet. However, follow along to see the kind of changes you can make.

⑫ Specify the background color or image for the `#mainMenu` selector.

Adjust the background color or image as needed to match your HTML page design.

In the book example, I could use either a background color of `#1D6963` or an image. However, the 756 x 30px image I created in Photoshop in Chapter 2 makes for a seamless transition between the background of my `header div` element and the menu itself.

⑬ Specify the background color for the `#mainMenu .activeMenuItem` selector.

Locate the `#mainMenu .activeMenuItem` selector in the stylesheet and set its background color to something that contrasts with the background color or image you set in Step 12.

For the book example, I set it to `#59A09A`.

⑭ Specify the background color for the `#submenu` selector.

The `#submenu` selector defines the formatting for the `submenu div` that appears just

Creating a Top-Level Menu Bar *(continued)*

below the `mainMenu div`. Locate the selector in your stylesheet code and then alter the background color as needed.

The book example uses the hex color code #59A09A, which complements the background used in the `mainMenu div`.

⓯ If needed, adjust the color style in the `#mainMenu`, `#mainMenu a`, `#submenu`, **and** `#mainMenu.inactiveMenuItem` **selectors.**

The font color is initially set to white in the `tabmenu.css` stylesheet. However, if the colors you selected in Steps 12–14 are light, you may need to darken the font color.

⓰ Save the changes to your CSS stylesheet.

Choose File↷Save in Dreamweaver.

⓱ View the new menu bar in your browser.

After you save changes to the stylesheet, open your HTML page in a browser to view the final results of the makeover.

The book's example file for this makeover is `makeover_03_02.html`.

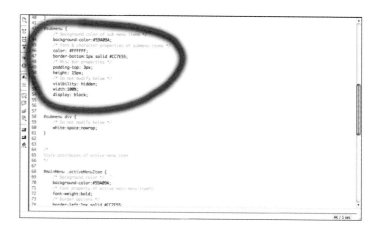

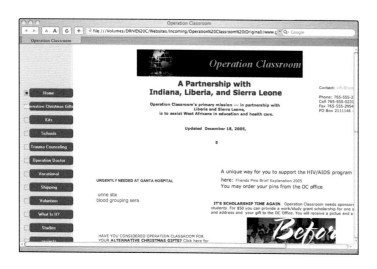

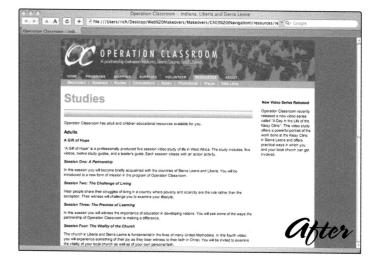

Creating a Vertical Navigation List

A horizontal menu bar at the top of an HTML page is the most ubiquitous navigational tool on the Web. However, a second common method is a vertical navigation list or menu, located either on the left or right column of the page.

In some cases, this vertical list complements the existing top-level menu, while in other cases, it can be used instead of a horizontal menu.

A vertical menu is often just a fancy name for an ordinary HTML bulleted list. However, as this makeover shows, you can transform an unordered list into something much more effective and visually appealing by using CSS formatting.

In this makeover, you discover how to transform a "plain Jane" HTML bulleted list into a stylish vertical menu. (Not sure what *plain* means in this context? Check out the bullet list on the right side of the Web page shown here.)

Note: Before starting, be sure you download `navlist.css` from the book's Web site and copy it into your css subfolder.

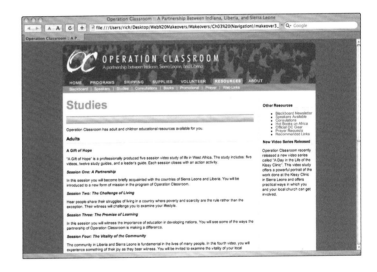

❶ Open an HTML page to which you wish to add a vertical navigation list.

In Dreamweaver, choose File⇨Open.

If you're following along with the book example, the vertical menu will be used to highlight the associated submenu items related to the current page. Start with the `makeover_03_03.html` file.

❷ View the HTML code for the page.

In Dreamweaver, click the Code button on the Document toolbar.

❸ Add a link element in your document header connecting the `navlist.css` **stylesheet with your HTML page.**

Type the following code in your document header:

```
<link rel="stylesheet"
rev="stylesheet"
href="css/navlist.css"
type="text/css" media="screen"
charset="utf-8" />
```

The `navlist.css` code provides all of the formatting you'll need for your navigation list.

❹ Inside the `rightColumn` **div, add a new** `navlist` **div.**

The `navlist` `div` will contain the navigation list and its heading. Type the following:

```
<div id="navlist">
</div>
```

❺ Enter a bulleted list of a elements.

Using an unordered list structure, enter a list of a elements that link to the pages you'd like to list in the vertical menu. For example:

```
<ul>
<li><a href="resources/black-
board.html">Blackboard
Newsletter</a></li>
</ul>
```

If you're using the book example, enter the links as shown to the right.

❻ Add an h2 **heading to the navigation list.**

Here's your chance to give the navigation list a descriptive title.

❼ Save changes to your HTML page.

Choose File⇨Save in Dreamweaver.

```
1   <!DOCTYPE HTML PUBLIC "-//W3C//DTD HTML 4.01//EN" "http://www.w3.org/TR/html4/strict.dtd">
2   <html>
3   <head>
4   <title>Operation Classroom :: A Partnership Between Indiana, Liberia, and Sierra Leone</title>
5   <link rel="stylesheet" rev="stylesheet" href="css/ocglobal.css" type="text/css" media="screen" charset="utf-8" />
6   <link rel="stylesheet" rev="stylesheet" href="css/tabmenu.css" type="text/css" media="screen" charset="utf-8" />
7   <link rel="stylesheet" rev="stylesheet" href="css/navlist.css" type="text/css" media="screen" charset="utf-8" />
8   <script src="css/tabmenu.js" type="text/javascript" language="Javascript1.2" charset="utf-8"></script>
9   </head>
10  <body>
11  <div id="topBorder"> </div>
12  <div id="header"></div>
13  <div id="container">
14  <div id="mainMenu">
15      <a class="inactiveMenuItem" style="left: 15px;" id="mainMenuItem1" href="index.html">Home</a>
16      <a class="inactiveMenuItem" style="left: 110px;" id="mainMenuItem2" href="../programs/programs.html">Programs</a>
17      <a class="inactiveMenuItem" style="left: 195px;" id="mainMenuItem3" href="../shipping/shipping.html">Shipping</a>
18      <a class="inactiveMenuItem" style="left: 280px;" id="mainMenuItem4" href="../supplies/supplies.html">Supplies</a>
19      <a class="inactiveMenuItem" style="left: 365px;" id="mainMenuItem5" href="../volunteer/volunteer.html">Volunteer</a>
20      <a class="activeMenuItem" style="left: 450px;" id="mainMenuItem6" href="../resources/resources.html">Resources</a>
21      <a class="inactiveMenuItem" style="left: 535px;" id="mainMenuItem7" href="../about/about.html">About</a>
22  </div>
23  <div id="submenu">
24      <div style="padding-left: 15px; position: static; display: none;" id="submenu_1">
25      </div>
26      <div style="padding-left: 15px; position: static; display: none;" id="submenu_2">
27          <a href="../programs/schools.html">Schools</a> |
28          <a href="../programs/vocational.html">Vocational</a> |
29          <a href="../programs/training.html">WATTS</a> |
30          <a href="../programs/medical.html">Operation Doctor</a>
31      </div>
32      <div style="padding-left: 15px; position: static; display: none;" id="submenu_3">
33          <a href="../shipping/hosts.html">Instructions</a> |
```
`9K / 2 sec`

```
54          <a href="../resources/links.html">Web Links</a>
55      </div>
56      <div style="padding-left: 15px; position: static; display: none;" id="submenu_7">
57          <a href="../about/contactus.html">Contact Us</a> |
58          <a href="../about/history.html">History</a>
59      </div>
60  </div>
61  <div id="rightColumn">
62  <div id="navlist">
63  <ul>
64  <li><a href="resources/blackboard.html">Blackboard Newsletter</a></li>
65  <li><a href="resources/speakers.html">Speakers Available</a></li>
66  <li><a href="resources/consultations.html">Consultations</a></li>
67  <li><a href="resources/books.html">Hot Books on Africa</a></li>
68  <li><a href="resources/ocgear.html">Official OC Gear</a></li>
69  <li><a href="resources/prayer.html">Prayer Requests</a></li>
70  <li><a href="resources/links.html">Recommended Links</a></li>
71  </ul>
72  </div>
73  <h2>New Video Series Released </h2>
74  <p>
75  Operation Classroom recently released a new video series called &quot;A Day in the Life of the Kissy Clinic&quot;. This video
    study offers a powerful portrait of the work done at the Kissy Clinic in Sierra Leone and offers practical ways in which you and
    your local community can get involved. </p>
76  </div>
77
78  <div id="content">
79  <div id="pagetitle">Studies</div>
80  <div id="pagetitlespacer"></div>
81
82  <p>Operation Classroom has adult and children educational resources available for you. </p>
83  <h2><strong>Adults</strong></h2>
```
`9K / 2 sec`

```
61  <div id="rightColumn">
62  <div id="navlist">
63  <h2>Other Resources</h2>
64  <ul>
65  <li><a href="resources/blackboard.html">Blackboard Newsletter</a></li>
66  <li><a href="resources/speakers.html">Speakers Available</a></li>
67  <li><a href="resources/consultations.html">Consultations</a></li>
68  <li><a href="resources/books.html">Hot Books on Africa</a></li>
69  <li><a href="resources/ocgear.html">Official OC Gear</a></li>
70  <li><a href="resources/prayer.html">Prayer Requests</a></li>
71  <li><a href="resources/links.html">Recommended Links</a></li>
72  </ul>
73  </div>
74  <h2>New Video Series Released </h2>
75  <p>
76  Operation Classroom recently released a new video series called &quot;A Day in the Life of the Kissy Clinic&quot;. This video
    study offers a powerful portrait of the work done at the Kissy Clinic in Sierra Leone and offers practical ways in which you and
    your local community can get involved. </p>
77  </div>
78
79  <div id="content">
80  <div id="pagetitle">Studies</div>
81  <div id="pagetitlespacer"></div>
82
83  <p>Operation Classroom has adult and children educational resources available for you. </p>
84  <h2><strong>Adults</strong></h2>
85  <hr>
86  <p><strong>A Gift of Hope</strong></p>
87  <p>&quot;A Gift of Hope&quot; is a professionally produced five session video study of life in West Africa. The study includes:
    five videos, twelve study guides, and a leader's guide. Each session closes with an action activity.</p>
88  <p><em> Session One: A Partnership in Mission</em></p>
89  <p> In this session you will become briefly acquainted with the countries of Sierra Leone and Liberia. You will be introduced to a
    new form of mission in the process of Operation Classroom. </p>
```
`9K / 2 sec`

⑧ Open the `navlist.css` file.

Choose File⇨Open and select `navlist.css` to open for editing inside of Dreamweaver.

The `navlist.css` stylesheet sets the formatting for your navigation list.

If you're following along with the book example, you don't need to make any changes to `navlist.css`.

⑨ Adjust the background style in the `#navlist h2` selector.

If needed, change the background color to a color that matches your Web site color scheme.

⑩ If needed, adjust the background style in other selectors.

The colors used for the list items are shades of gray, so you may not need to make any changes. However, feel free to tweak to a color scheme that works best for your Web site.

⑪ Save changes to the `navlist.css` stylesheet.

Choose File⇨Save in Dreamweaver.

⑫ View the new navigation list in your browser.

After you've saved changes to the stylesheet, go ahead and open up your HTML page in a browser to view the makeover.

The book's example file for this makeover is `makeover_03_03.html`.

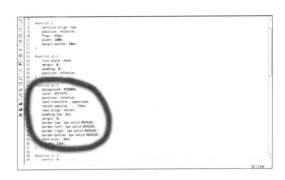

Adding a Pathway to Your Pages

Lost in a world of hypertext? That's one of the natural reactions visitors may experience when they go to your site, even if you take great pains to structure your site clearly and logically.

One way you can prevent disorientation is to provide "bread crumbs" — or a pathway — that help users navigate through your steps. Here, the pathway is a horizontal list of links that show how a given page fits into the Web site's hierarchy. For example, a Books page that is in the Resources section of a site would have a pathway that looks like:

```
Home > Resources > Books
```

Not only does the pathway provide a visual indicator of a visitor's context in your Web site, but it also provides quick links to "move up" the site hierarchy.

Follow the steps below to add a pathway to your Web site.

① Open an HTML page to which you wish to add a pathway.

In Dreamweaver, choose File⇨Open.

If you're working through the book examples, open `makeover_03_04.html`.

② View the HTML code for the page.

In Dreamweaver, click the Code button on the Document toolbar.

③ Add a new `pathway` `div` **element inside your page's** `content` `div`.

The `pathway` `div` element houses the pathway text. Locate your page's `content` `div` element and add an empty `div` element (before the `pagetitle` `div`):

```
<div id="pathway"> </div>
```

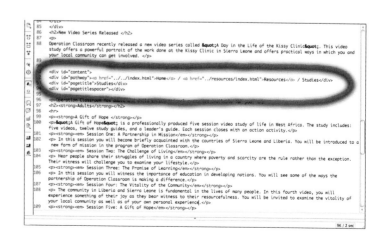

④ Inside the `pathway` **div, add the hierarchical pathway to your page.**

Starting from the home page, add each page title in the hierarchy as an a element (a link) until you get to the current page, separating each with a > or / symbol and surrounding spaces.

For the current page, add the text only, with no link.

⑤ Save changes to your HTML page.

Choose File⇨Save in Dreamweaver.

⑥ Open the CSS stylesheet that is linked to your Web page.

In Dreamweaver, choose File⇨Open.

You want to define CSS formatting to style your pathway.

⑦ Add a new `#pathway` **selector to your stylesheet.**

The `#pathway` selector sets both the `div` element formatting as well as the text inside of it.

If you're working through the book examples, add the rule shown on the right.

⑧ Save changes to the stylesheet.

Choose File⇨Save in Dreamweaver.

⑨ View the pathway inside your browser.

Open your HTML page in a browser to view the final results of the makeover.

The book's example file for this makeover is `makeover_03_04.html`.

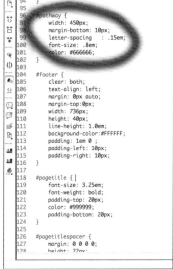

Adding a Quick Links Drop-Down Menu

Web site navigation is usually best achieved through horizontal and vertical menus, such as the ones discussed in this chapter. Another technique that can be effective in certain circumstances, however, is a drop-down list menu. While I don't recommend a drop-down menu as suitable for your site's primary navigation, it *can* be especially useful for quick links to commonly requested pages in your site.

If you'd like to add this drop-down menu to your site, check out this makeover.

① Open an HTML page to which you wish to add the drop-down menu.

In Dreamweaver, choose File⇨Open.

If you're working with the book examples, open the `makeover_03_05.html` file.

② View the HTML code for the page.

In Dreamweaver, click the Code button on the Document toolbar.

③ Add a new `quickLinks` div element inside the `rightColumn` div.

The new `div` will contain the drop-down select list, its header, and some JavaScript. The basic structure is as follows:

```
<div id="quickLinks">
</div>
```

④ Inside the `quickLinks` div, add a form element named `quickLinksForm`.

The `form` element will contain the `select` list.

❺ Add an `h2` heading inside the form.

Just after the opening `form` tag, add the following:

```
<h2>Quick Links:</h2>
```

❻ Add a `select` element named `quickLinksList` inside the form.

For the first `option` element in the list, add the following:

```
<option value=""> I want to...
```

This text will appear as the default list item.

Then, for each link you'd like to add to the list, assign its URL to the `value` attribute and add the desired text that you wish to appear for the list item outside of the element's tag.

If you're working with the example from the book, enter the code as shown on the right.

❼ Add an `onChange` event handler to the select list.

In order for the drop-down list to actually jump to a new page, you need to script this functionality. As a first step, add the following event handler to the `select` definition:

```
onChange="gotoLink()"
```

A JavaScript routine named `gotoLink()` will be called whenever the `select` element's value changes.

❽ Add JavaScript inside the `quickLinks` div.

The following script tells the browser to change the URL location it's pointing to based on the current `option` value in the `select` list:

```
<script language="JavaScript"
type="text/javascript">
function gotoLink() {
    if
(document.quickLinksForm.quickLi
nksList.options[document.quickLi
nksForm.quickLinksList.selectedI
ndex].value != "") {
        location =
document.quickLinksForm.quickLin
ksList.options[document.quickLin
ksForm.quickLinksList.selectedIn
dex].value
    }
}
</script>
```

⑨ Save the changes to your HTML page.

Choose File⇨Save from the menu in Dreamweaver.

⑩ Open the CSS stylesheet that is linked to your Web page.

Choose File⇨Open from the Dreamweaver menu.

You add CSS rules in the stylesheet to format your drop-down menu.

⑪ Add a new `#quickLinks select` **selector to your stylesheet.**

The `#quickLinks select` selector sets the formatting for the quick link `select` element you just defined.

Enter the width, margin, and font settings as specified below, adjusting the color to fit your site's color scheme:

```
#quickLinks select {
    width: 145px;
    margin :  0px 0px 1em 0px;
    font: 90%/1em Arial,
Helvetica, sans-serif;
    color: #CC7E55;
}
```

```
70
71  <div id="rightColumn">
72
73  <script language="JavaScript" type="text/javascript">
74  function gotoLink() {
75      if (document.quickLinksForm.quickLinksList.options[document.quickLinksForm.quickLinksList.selectedIndex].value != "") {
76          location = document.quickLinksForm.quickLinksList.options[document.quickLinksForm.quickLinksList.selectedIndex].value
77      }
78  }
79  </script>
80  <form name="quickLinksForm">
81  <h2>Quick Links:</h2>
82  <select name="quickLinksList" onChange="gotoLink()">
83  <option value=""> I want to...
84  <option value="../shipping/instructions.html"> Ship supplies overseas
85  <option value="../volunteer/index.html"> Volunteer for a workteam
86  <option value="../shipping/shipform.html"> Download a shipping Form
87  <option value="../resources/speakers.html"> Request a speaker
88  <option value="../about/index.html"> Learn more about OC
89  </select>
90  </form>
91  </div>
92  <div id="navlist">
93  <h2>Other Resources</h2>
94  <ul>
95  <li><a href="#">Blackboard Newsletter</a></li>
96  <li><a href="#">Speakers Available</a></li>
97  <li><a href="#">Consulations</a></li>
98  <li><a href="#">Hot Books on Africa</a></li>
99  <li><a href="#">Official OC Gear</a></li>
100 <li><a href="#">Prayer Requests</a></li>
101 <li><a href="#">Recommended Links</a></li>
```

10K / 2 sec

⑫ Add a new #quickLinks h2 selector to your stylesheet.

The #quickLinks h2 selector defines the formatting for your h2 heading inside the quickLinks div. Enter text as follows:

```
#quickLinks h2 {
    font-weight: normal;
    padding-left: 2px;
    margin-bottom: 10px;
    line-height: .1em;
    border: none;
}
```

⑬ Save changes to the stylesheet.

Choose File⇨Save in Dreamweaver.

⑭ View the drop-down menu list inside your browser.

Open your HTML page in a browser to view the final results of the makeover.

The book's example file for this makeover is makeover_03_05.html.

Before

After

4

PAGE ELEMENT MAKEOVERS

Even after you work hard designing a killer page layout for your pages, you can't just drop in text, images, tables, and other elements and expect it to look good. Instead, you need to pay close attention to the look of each element on your page and how all the page elements coexist to form a unified design.

This chapter explores several makeovers to help you transform the ordinary into the extraordinary. You begin by looking at how tweaking the properties of an HTML table changes it from looking like every other table out there into something that complements your overall page design. You then make over a crowded arrangement of elements, using different CSS tricks to make sure each element stands alone yet plays well with others. Next up, you turn your focus to two makeovers involving a designer's *wunderkind* element — the iframe.

Enhancing the Look of Table Borders

Though they often are, tables don't have to be ugly. I don't know who came up with the default HTML raised-borders table look, but I always thought it looked cheesy. When I stumble across a site that uses it today, I feel like I'm back in the mid-90s. Unfortunately, many people building Web pages accept the default table look — shown here in all its glory in the neighboring column — as a fact of life.

Here's a makeover to change all that.

① Open an HTML page that contains a table you wish to make over.

In Dreamweaver, you choose File⇨Open.

If you're working with the book examples, open the `makeover_04_01.html` file.

② In Design view, select the table you are going to modify.

Click inside any of the table cells and then click the appropriate table element in the element hierarchy, shown on the Dreamweaver status bar.

For the book example, click in a cell inside the Senior Division table and then click the `table#Table1` button on the status bar.

The entire table is selected, and the Properties palette is updated to reflect the table's properties.

③ Change the `CellPad` to 1, `CellSpace` to 1, and `Border` to 0.

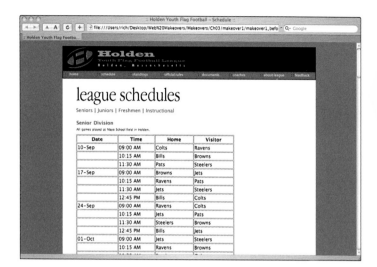

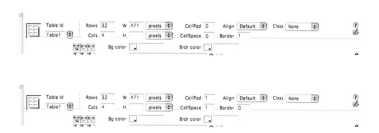

These property changes remove the border and add some space inside and between the cells.

④ Select the first row of the table.

As you hover the mouse over the left side of the Date cell, the mouse cursor changes to an arrow. Click to select the entire row.

⑤ Enter a background color for the header row in the Bg property box in the Properties bar.

For the book example, type #000000. As the example file shows, black serves as a great general column header color for a variety of color schemes.

⑥ Enter #ffffff (or another contrasting color) as the text color property in the Properties bar.

Unless you selected a light background color, you usually want to choose white (#ffffff) as the heading text color.

⑦ Select the rest of the cells of your table.

In Dreamweaver, click and drag your mouse to select all of the other table cells. Make sure that you don't select the header row you just adjusted.

⑧ Enter a background color for the table cells in the Properties bar's Bg box.

The book example uses a dark gray, which has a hex color code of #b3b3b5.

If you need to, adjust the text color property as well in the Property bar.

Enhancing the Look of Table Borders *(continued)*

⑨ Save changes to your HTML page.

Choose File⇨Save in Dreamweaver.

⑩ View your made-over table in your browser.

In Dreamweaver, click the Preview/Debug in Browser button on the Document toolbar and select the desired browser from the list. Your page opens in the browser you selected.

Offsetting Page Elements to Avoid Eye Competition

Web-based communication is something like talking with your spouse. It's not just what you say, but also how you say it.

Although your Web site is designed to communicate information to interested visitors, never expect people to start at the top left and thoroughly read everything until they get to the bottom right. They're going to scan headlines, reading bits and pieces. If you aren't careful, you can create a Web page that is difficult for people to read because it goes against their reading habits. Crowded pages — like the one shown to the right — prevent scanning, create a feeling of claustrophobia, and earn you a quick Back-button click from their browsers.

Check out this makeover that creates an inviting Web page for your visitors to inhabit.

Note: The best way in which to offset content is unique to every situation. In this makeover, I focus on a variety of techniques. For your Web page, use the ones that make sense in your context.

In addition, this makeover assumes the `div`-based, two-column layout that is explored in Chapter 2.

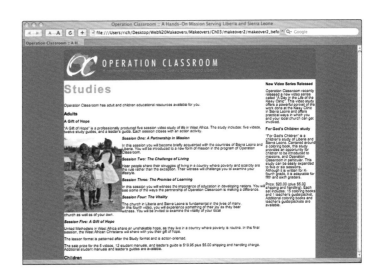

① **Open the CSS stylesheet that contains the HTML page's formatting instructions.**

Each of the offsetting techniques in this makeover is accomplished through CSS.

In Dreamweaver, choose File⇨Open to open the CSS stylesheet.

If you are using the book's example files, open the `makeover_04_02.css` file.

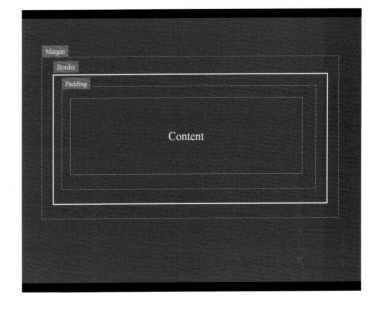

Offsetting Page Elements to Avoid Eye Competition *(continued)*

② **In the #content selector, add padding and right-margin rules.**

In your HTML page, the content div contains your main text body. However, it shares real estate in the container div with the rightColumn div, which is used to display sidebar information.

Currently, the rightColumn div wraps around the content div but doesn't take up an entire vertical column. Therefore, when rightColumn div content ends, the content div flows back underneath it. However, to ensure that the content div doesn't extend into the region in which rightColumn inhabits, you need to add a margin-right rule:

```
margin-right: 175px;
```

This rule indents the content div 175 pixels from the right edge of the container div. And because the rightColumn is 150 pixels wide, this rule ensures that (1) the content div gives the entire right-hand side to the rightColumn to do its own thing, and (2) the content div always has 25 pixels of whitespace between it and rightColumn.

In addition, add a padding rule to offset the text inside the content div from its borders. Using em as a measurement unit is optimal because, as Chapter 5 discusses, the

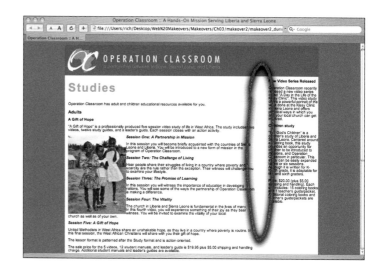

em adjusts its size based on the relative font size. Here's the second rule to add:

```
padding: 1em;
```

❸ In the `#rightColumn` selector, add margin, padding, and border rules.

While the offset between the `content div` and the `rightColumn div` is already taken care of by `content`'s CSS rules, we can further divide the two regions of the page by adding a border on the left side of the `div`. A gray, dotted border seems consistent with the overall style. Here's the rule:

```
border-left: 1px dotted #cccccc;
```

However, to separate the border from the content inside of the `div`, you need to add padding:

```
padding: 1em;
```

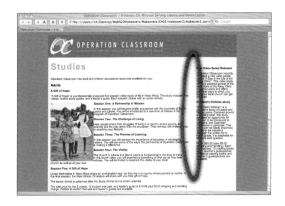

To ensure the border extends beyond the content of the `div` itself, you can add a rule that specifies a minimum height for the `div`:

```
min-height: 600px;
```

Next, to add some whitespace at the top of the column, you should add a top margin rule:

```
margin-top: 20px;
```

❹ In the `#rightColumn h2` selector, add margin, padding, and border rules.

The `h2` headings in the `rightColumn div` should be visually offset from the normal paragraph text.

Begin by adding a bottom margin and border to separate the heading from its content:

```
margin-bottom: 10px;
border-bottom: 1px dotted
#cccccc;
```

You should also add padding between the `h2` text and the border:

```
padding-bottom: 3px;
```

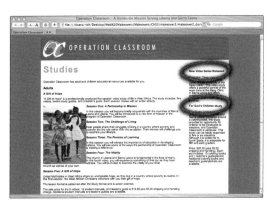

Offsetting Page Elements to Avoid Eye Competition *(continued)*

⑤ In the `#rightColumn h2` **selector, add a background image to help make the h2 headings stand out.**

While the margin and border help, one final technique you can use to make the headings stand out involves placing a small image at the start of the line. Use the following code:

```
background-image:
url('../images/darrow.gif');
background-position: top left;
background-repeat: no-repeat;
padding-left: 12px;
```

These rules set `darrow.gif` as a background image in the top-left position of the h2 space. A padding rule is added to ensure there is enough space between the image and the start of the text.

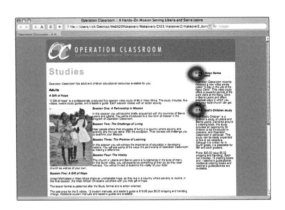

⑥ In the `p` **selector, increase the line height to 1.35em.**

To make the text on the entire page easier to read, add the following line to the p selector:

```
line-height: 1.35em;
```

The net effect is a much roomier page.

You're almost finished. However, you need to offset any images on the page from the paragraph text. The offset settings for images usually depend on their specific placement, so you'll probably want to adjust their properties inside the HTML page itself. Before you do that, however, you should choose File⇨Save to save changes to your CSS stylesheet.

⑦ Open your HTML page.

Choose File⇨Open in Dreamweaver.

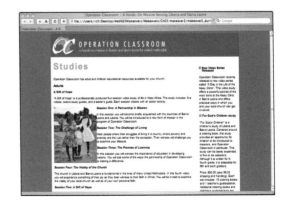

If you're working with the book example, choose `makeover_04_02.html`.

⑧ In Design view, select the image you wish to offset.

For the book example, you'll want to select the image of the three school children.

⑨ Click the Split button on the Document toolbar so you can simultaneously work with the img element's code.

The Split view is handy when you need to work with the code and visual design at the same time.

⑩ Add a style tag to provide off-set instructions.

Although you can offset an img element by using vspace and hspace attributes, CSS rules give you more control.

Take our book example as one case study. The image is left-aligned. You could add an hspace value to offset the text around it, but the downside is that the image is now indented from the left margin. However, if you add an in-place style rule, you can adjust the margin for just the right side:

```
style="margin-right: 10px;"
```

If you're working with the book example, adjust the border color as well:

```
style="margin-right: 10px;
border-color=#cccccc"
```

⑪ Save changes to your HTML page.

Choose File⮑Save in Dreamweaver.

⑫ To view your made-over page, click the Preview/Debug in Browser button on your Document toolbar and then select your favorite browser from the list.

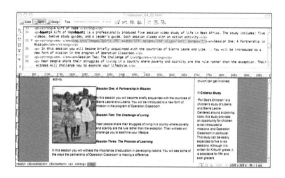

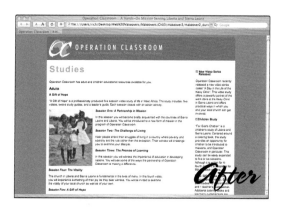

Using iframes to Package Your Content

Imagine you've come up with a great fixed page layout that works perfectly for your Web site needs. However, after all your hard work, suppose you discover that the amount of text your fixed page needs to handle ends up being more than twice what you planned — something like the situation you see here to the right. In the early years of the Web, you'd either have to use kludgy frames or else redesign the page. However, by using an iframe — or, an inline frame, which is much like a page within a page — you can place a variable amount of text in a fixed portion of your page.

Here's how to package your content with an iframe.

➊ Open the HTML page to which you wish to add an iframe.

In Dreamweaver, choosing File➪Open does the trick.

The book example file for this makeover is makeover_04_03.html.

➋ Select and then cut the text you wish to put into an iframe.

In Dreamweaver's Design view, you select the text and then choose Edit➪Cut.

➌ Create a new blank HTML page into which you'll insert your cut text.

In Dreamweaver, choose File➪New and then choose HTML from the Basic page list. Click the Create button to finish the task.

④ Paste the cut text into your new HTML page.

Dreamweaver makes it easy; just choose Edit↷Paste.

⑤ Set the background color to match the color of the original HTML page.

In Dreamweaver, choose Modify↷Page Properties to call up the Page Properties dialog box. (You set the background color in the Appearance region of the dialog box.)

If you're working through the book example, enter #000000 in the Background color's hex code box and then click OK.

⑥ Click the Code button on the Document toolbar to view the HTML code.

⑦ Link any necessary stylesheets into your new HTML page.

To maintain consistent formatting, be sure to link your site's stylesheet to your page.

⑧ Save the HTML page.

Choose File↷Save to save your new HTML page.

If you're working with the book example, name it `power_details.html`.

⑨ Return to your original HTML page.

If you're in Dreamweaver, click the page's Document tab.

If you're working with the book example, you'll actually open a different sample file instead. That's because, with the additional space gained by adding an iframe, I am free to add some graphical elements to the page (which, come to think of it, is another great advantage to using iframes). Open `makeover_04_03_iframe.html`.

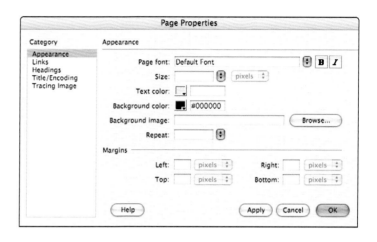

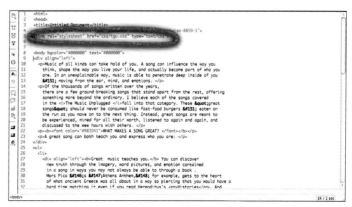

Using iframes to Package Your Content *(continued)*

⑩ Position your cursor where you want to place your iframe.

If you're not in Split view in Dreamweaver, click the Split button on the Document toolbar.

If you're working through the book example, position your cursor in the blank space below the "Great Music" caption.

⑪ In the Code view, add an iframe element.

The `iframe` element is a rectangular block that brings in the contents from another URL.

Here's the code I use for the book example. You'll want to adjust the `width` and `height` to meet your specific needs:

```
<iframe src="power_details.html"
align="top" width=370 height=350
marginwidth=30 marginheight=0
hspace=0 vspace=0 frameborder=0
scrolling=yes></iframe>
```

The `scrolling` attribute causes a scroll bar to appear when the contents of the referenced page extend beyond the `iframe` dimensions.

⑫ Save your changes.

As always, choose File➪Save in Dreamweaver to make your changes permanent.

⑬ View your makeover in your default browser by clicking the Preview/Debug in Browser button on the Document toolbar and selecting your favorite browser.

Bringing iframes to Life

iframes are a great solution to the problem of variable text within a fixed space. But the iframe's scroll bars bring a dose of "browser reality" to an otherwise cool page design. (Such a dose of reality can be seen in the page to the right.) You can always hide the offending scroll bars, but that's impractical if your text extends beyond the size of the iframe dimensions. However, here's a makeover that enables you to control the scrolling of your iframe — with controls that match your design.

1 Open the HTML page containing your iframe.

In Dreamweaver, choose File⇨Open to open your file.

If you are working through the book examples, use `makeover_04_04.html`.

2 View the HTML code of your document.

If you're in Dreamweaver, click the Code button on the Document toolbar.

3 Locate the `iframe` element inside your file.

If you are working with the book example, look for the HTML comment tag `<!-TGU CONTENT SECTION START -->`.

4 Add a `div` element just below the iframe element.

The `div` element will house your custom scrolling controls.

In a style tag, set its width to be identical to the width of the iframe. Next, add a small top margin to offset its content from the iframe. Finally, set its alignment to `right`. Here's the `div` element's code:

```
<div style="width:370px;margin-
top:3px;" margin-right:5px;
align="right">
</div>
```

Bringing iframes to Life *(continued)*

⑤ Inside the `div` element, wrap an `img` element inside an `a` element to serve as the scroll-up control.

Clickable images can serve as ideal controls for managing the scrolling of the iframe. Begin by adding a scroll-up arrow image. Enter this code:

```
<a href="#" onMouseover=
"scrollspeed=-1" onMouseout=
"scrollspeed=0"><img
SRC="images/uarw.gif"
border="0"></a>
```

You define a null link (`href="#"`) because you don't actually want to link to another Web page.

For the `onMouseover` event handler, set the browser window's `scrollspeed` to `-1` and then reset the `scrollspeed` to `0` for the `onMouseout` handler.

The `img` references any image that represents an up arrow. You can find `uarrow.gif` and `uarw.gif` on the book's Web site.

⑥ Add a second `img` element wrapped inside an `a` element as the scroll-down control.

The only difference in the code is that the `onMouseover` `scrollspeed` value is a positive value that corresponds with the value you placed in the `up arrow` element. In addition, the `img` element references an image that displays a down arrow. (You can find `darrow.gif` and `darw.gif` on the book's Web site.)

Here's the code:

```
<a href="#" onMouseover=
"scrollspeed=1" onMouseout=
"scrollspeed=0"><img SRC="images/
darw.gif" border="0"></a>
```

⑦ Save changes to your HTML page.

Choosing File➪Save from the menu will do the trick.

⑧ Open the HTML page that is referenced by the iframe.

Choose File➪Open in Dreamweaver.

If you're working through the example makeover, open power_details.html.

⑨ View the HTML code of your document.

If you're using Dreamweaver, click the Code button on the Document toolbar.

⑩ In the document head, add a link to the scroller.js external JavaScript file.

The scroller.js file is a JavaScript script included on the book's Web site that provides all the code needed to give life to the up and down arrows that you previously added to your page. You just need to link this external scripting file into your iframe-referenced Web page. (Make sure you copy this file into your css folder.)

Type this code:

```
<script language="JavaScript1.2"
src="css/scroller.js"></script>
```

⑪ Save changes to your HTML page.

From your menu, choose File➪Save.

⑫ Try out your new scrolling buttons in your browser.

Click back to the HTML page containing your iframe element, click the Preview/Debug in Browser button on the Document toolbar, and then select a browser from the pop-up list.

Take a look at the results of your makeover in your default browser.

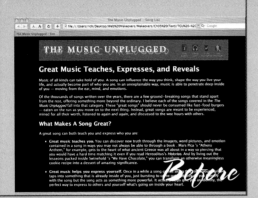

THE MUSIC UNPLUGGED

Great Music Teaches, Expresses, and Reveals

Music of all kinds can take hold of you. A song can influence the way you think, shape the way you live your life, and actually become part of who you are. In an unexplainable way, music is able to penetrate deep inside of you — moving from the ear, mind, and emotions.

Of the thousands of songs written over the years, there are a few ground-breaking songs that stand apart from the rest, offering something more beyond the ordinary. I believe each of the songs covered in the *The Music Unplugged* fall into that category. These "great songs" should never be consumed like fast-food burgers — eaten on the run as you move on to the next thing. Instead, great songs are meant to be experienced, mined for all their worth, listened to again and again, and discussed to the wee hours with others.

What Makes A Song Great?

A great song can both teach you and express who you are:

- **Great music teaches you.** You can discover new truth through the imagery, word pictures, and emotion contained in a song in ways you may not always be able to through a book . Mars Pica 's "Athens Anthem," for example, gets to the heart of what ancient Greece was all about in a way so piercing that you would have a hard time matching it even if you read Hereoditus's *Histories*. And by living out the lesseons packed inside Swinehold 's "We Have Chocolate," you can transform an otherwise meaningless cookie recipe into a dessert of amazing significance.

- **Great music helps you express yourself.** Once in a while a song comes along that rocks your world and taps into something that is already inside of you, just bursting to come out. Not only do you identify with the song but the song acts as something more powerful. It actually helps give you an identity, the perfect way to express to others and yourself what's going on inside your heart.

Before

After

5 TEXT MAKEOVERS

When you place text on your Web site, you should have a dual goal of readability and visual appeal. You want to present written information clearly to your visitors, but you want to do so in a manner that complements your site design, rather than detracting from it. The key is striking an appropriate balance between these two objectives.

In this chapter, you examine three text-oriented makeovers that help you achieve your design goals without sacrificing readability. The first makeover shows you how to take charge of your site's fonts through CSS. You then examine a makeover that takes an ordinary text heading and transforms it into something special by making it a graphic. Finally, bulleted lists are one of the popular ways to present lists of information. I show you how to change ordinary HTML bullets into the image bullet you specify.

Selecting Fonts that Complement Your Site

Because text is perhaps the most dominant component of any Web site, you should not leave the font in which the text is presented to chance. Fonts alone will, of course, never make a killer Web site design, but neglecting them can significantly diminish the overall appeal of your efforts. (The page you see here to the right, for example, could use some font work.)

The following makeover transforms the fonts of a page to complement the page's design goals.

❶ Open the CSS stylesheet that is linked to your Web page.

You want to define all of your font styles by using CSS, giving you maximum flexibility across your Web site.

If you're following along with the book examples, open `makeover_05_01.css`.

If you aren't using an external stylesheet, you want to define your styles inside a `style` element in the document header.

Note: If you are applying this makeover to an existing HTML page, check the source code first for existing `font` tags. After making a backup of your original, you'll want to clean house and get rid of the existing font formatting instructions.

❷ Add a `font-family` declaration to the `body` selector.

The `font-family` declaration located in the `body` selector will set a default font for your Web site.

If you are following along with the book's example, enter the following line:

```
font-family: Arial, Helvetica,
sans-serif;
```

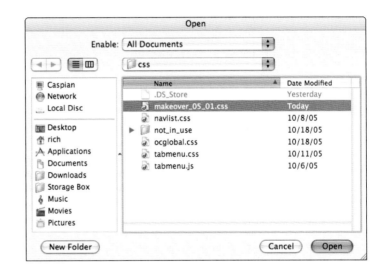

❸ Add two selectors to set the base font size for your Web site.

This makeover uses em units for fonts. An *em* is a unit of measurement that is relative to the current font. 1em is the size of the block that is needed to contain all of the characters in the font. Since a capital "M" is often the largest sized character in Latin-based alphabets, you can often think of 1em as the equivalent of the width of a capital "M." Therefore, when it comes to designing your Web page, you can think of 1em as equal to the capital "M" of the default browser font, which is usually set to "medium" text by users (which is 16 pixels in size). However, a 16-pixel font is simply too large for visually appealing, well-designed Web sites. Therefore, you need to reset the base font size to a lower number.

Selecting Fonts that Complement Your Site *(continued)*

To make things even more interesting, Internet Explorer for Windows deals with em measurements slightly differently than other browsers do, so when you use em units, you need to account for that disparity by adding the following code to your stylesheet:

```
body { font-size: 62.5%; }
/* Targets Internet Explorer -
Windows   */
html>body { font-size: 10px; }
/* Targets Other Browsers   */
```

Now that all browsers are in synch, you can think of 1em = 10px, 1.2 em = 12px, 1.6 em = 16px, and so on.

④ Add selectors that specify the relative font size for different parts of the page.

Now that the adjusted base font size has been set, you can set the size for each section of the page.

Here are the selectors I use for the book example:

```
#content       { font-size:
1.1em; }
#rightColumn { font-size:
1.0em; }
#pathway       { font-size:
0.8em; }
#footer        { font-size:
0.9em; }
#pagetitle     { font-size:
3.25em;}
#rightColumn h2 { font-size:
1em; }
#content h2 { font-size:
1.25em; }
```

```
 1   /**
 2    * Font Sizing
 3    * ---------------------
 4    */
 5
 6
 7   body { font-size: 62.5%; }          /* Enables all modern browsers to display em units */
 8   html>body { font-size: 10px; }      /* Targets Internet Explorer - Windows */
                                         /* Targets Other Browsers   */
11   /**
12    * General HTML Body Styling
13    * ---------------------
14    */
15
16   body {
17       font-family: Arial, Helvetica, sans-serif;
18       margin-top:0px;
19   }
20
21
22   p { line-height: 1.35em; }
23
24
25   /**
26    * Basic DIV Elements
27    * ---------------------
28    *
```

`4K / 1 sec`

```
 1   /**
 2    * Font Sizing
 3    * ---------------------
 4    */
 5
 6                                       /* Enables all modern browsers to display em units */
 7   body { font-size: 62.5%; }          /* Targets Internet Explorer - Windows */
 8   html>body { font-size: 10px; }      /* Targets Other Browsers */
 9
     #content       { font-size: 1.1em; }
     #rightColumn { font-size: 1.0em; }
     #pathway       { font-size: 0.8em; }
     #footer        { font-size: 0.9em; }
     #pagetitle     { font-size: 3.25em;}
     #rightColumn h2 { font-size: 1em; }
     #content h2 { font-size: 1.25em; }
17
18
19   /**
20    * General HTML Body Styling
21    * ---------------------
22    */
23
24   body {
25       font-family: Arial, Helvetica, sans-serif;
26       margin-top:0px;
27   }
28
```

`4K / 1 sec`

⑤ Choose File⇨Save to save your stylesheet.

You want to be sure and save your changes along the way.

⑥ View your new page look in your browser.

In your browser, open the HTML page to see how this makeover transforms your Web page.

The book's example file for this makeover is `makeover_05_01.html`.

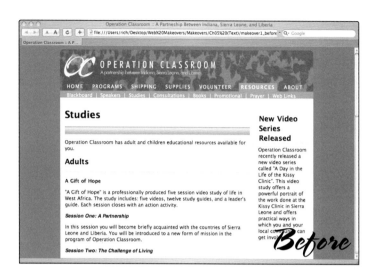

Font Sizing Options

The em unit is being recommended more and more as the best option for sizing your type. An em is considered user-friendly because it is relative to the font size of the user's default browser font. However, the downside is that your page layout can be skewed if the user chooses a default font size that's just too large.

Pixels are the most dependable solution when your layout needs to be precisely positioned, regardless of what the default browser font is set to. However, if someone wants to have your fonts enlarged for visibility reasons, your design doesn't adjust to their needs.

Points, which are perhaps the most popular font measurement in programs like Microsoft Word, are used less often in Web design because they can vary according to screen resolution.

Selecting Fonts that Complement Your Site *(continued)*

Rich's Take: Don't think of font selection and size as a last-minute detail or something that your visitors are solely responsible for through their browser preferences. The visual appeal of your text is an important design consideration and can make or break the look of your Web site. Consider, for example, the Before and After pictures to the right. Simply changing the `font-family` and `font-size` of the body text is the primary agent of change in this makeover.

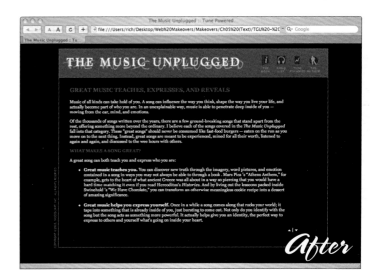

Replacing Normal Text with Anti-Aliased Text

On the Web, text often coexists alongside images. Text is for communicating the written word, while graphics are designed to convey visual information. (The page here to the right shows text sticking to its traditional task of conveying information simply and discretely.) However, on occasion, you may wish to cross over that barrier and display text as an image.

When you use a graphic to display text, you can use any font you like, without regard to what fonts your visitors may have installed. In addition, in Photoshop and other image software packages, you can *anti-alias* the text — smoothing the jagged edges of each character by subtly blending the text and background colors along the edge of the text.

Although displaying *all* of your Web site's text as an image is both impractical and usually undesirable, there are occasions in which it can transform an ordinary heading or even page of text into something more visually appealing.

Note: In the book's example, you'll notice that I keep the replacement image simple, using only text on a white background. Don't feel the need to go overboard when you replace text with an image. Because my page's navigational header already had an image overlay, I wanted to keep the image heading fairly simple to complement, rather than compete with, the existing design.

Here's a makeover that shows you how to do this.

① In Photoshop, choose File⇨New and create a new document (400x55px, 72 pixels/inch).

Choose whether you want the background to be white, another color, or transparent. For the book example, I chose white.

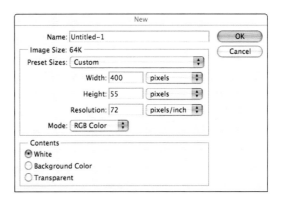

Replacing Normal Text with Anti-Aliased Text *(continued)*

② **Double-click the Foreground Color box in the Tools bar and choose a color for the text.**

If you are following along with the book example, enter **CC7E55** in the hex color box.

Click OK to close the Color Picker.

③ **Select the Horizontal Type tool from the Tools palette.**

Be sure you have the Horizontal Type tool selected and not the Vertical Type tool.

④ **Select font settings from the Options bar.**

For the book example, I use Ruach LET, 58pt and have anti-aliasing set to Crisp.

⑤ **In the Character palette, adjust the character tracking to 100.**

This option adds additional space between characters, which can be a subtle effect for page headings.

If your Character palette isn't visible, choose Window⇨Character from the Photoshop menu to bring it up onscreen.

⑥ **Type the name of the page heading on the document canvas.**

Type **Studies** for the book example.

⑦ **Save your working file.**

Although you later export this as a GIF file for use on your Web site, be sure to first save your working file in Photoshop's .PSD format — doing so enables you to easily make changes at a later time.

Choose File⇨Save and name the file **pageheading.psd** or another descriptive filename.

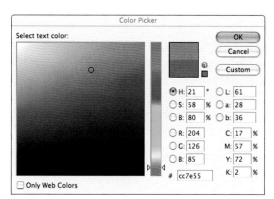

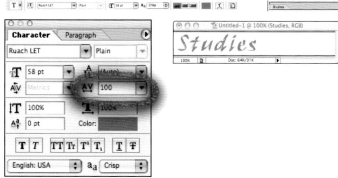

⑧ Save as a GIF file for use on your Web site.

Choose File➯Save For Web from the Photoshop menu.

Select GIF from the Optimized file format drop-down box.

⑨ Click the Save button in the Save For Web dialog box.

The Save Optimized As dialog box is displayed. Locate your images directory for your Web site, type **hd_studies.gif** in the Save As box, and click Save.

Your image heading is now ready to be added to your HTML page.

⑩ Open an HTML page whose heading text you wish to replace with an image.

In Dreamweaver, you choose File➯Open.

If you are working through the examples I've come up with, open makeover_05_02 .html. You'll replace the Studies text heading with an image.

⑪ View the HTML code for the page.

In Dreamweaver, click the Code button on the Document toolbar.

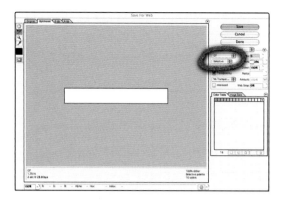

Replacing Normal Text with Anti-Aliased Text *(continued)*

⑫ Scroll down to the `pageheading` div **element.**

Back in the first chapter, you define a `page-heading div` to house the page heading text. You replace that text with an image.

⑬ Replace the text contents of the `div` **with an** `img` **element referencing your page heading image.**

Here's the code for the book example:

```
<img
src="images/header_class.gif"
alt="Studies" align="left">
```

Note: Be sure to add an `alt` attribute as a parameter to the `img` element. An `alt` attribute ensures that people who cannot or choose not to view images will have a text-based substitute. It is also a required attribute for XHTML documents (see Chapter 12).

⑭ (Optional) Remove the `pagetitlespacer` div **defined below the** `pageheading` div.

Because the heading text is now visually distinct from the body text, I chose to remove the title spacer originally defined in Chapter 1. I recommend you do the same.

⑮ Save changes to your HTML page.

Choose File⇨Save from the Dreamweaver menu.

⑯ Open the CSS stylesheet that contains the HTML page's formatting instructions.

Open the `makeover_05_02.css` file if you are using the book's example files.

⑰ Navigate down to the `#pageheading` **selector.**

Or, if you are using a stylesheet that doesn't contain an existing #pageheader selector, add it.

⑱ After removing the existing contents of the selector, add height and width definitions.

Specify a height of 55px and width of 756px.

⑲ Save changes to your CSS stylesheet.

Choose File⇨Save from the Dreamweaver menu.

Your makeover is now ready for viewing.

⑳ View your new page look in your browser.

You're ready for the best part of the makeover . . . seeing the results! Open the HTML page in your browser to view the final results of the makeover. If you are following along with the book's examples, open makeover_05_02.html.

Replacing Plain Bullets with Images

You may not have a shopping list or a to-do list on your Web site, but chances are, you've got other kinds of lists sprinkled all over your pages. A bulleted list is a great way to present information, though the ubiquitous round bullets in HTML are rather drab. (The ubiquitous round bullets are on display in the page on the right.)

In this makeover, I show you how to quickly transform normal bullets into images that you specify. Here's the scoop:

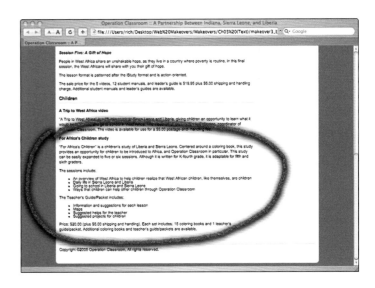

❶ Open the CSS stylesheet that contains the HTML page's formatting instructions.

By using CSS, you can modify the list bullets without even touching the actual lists in the HTML pages. You create selectors to customize the look of ul and li elements.

If you are using the book's example files, open the makeover_05_03.css file.

❷ Add a ul selector to the stylesheet.

In the stylesheet, add a ul selector to override the default presentation of unordered lists in your HTML page. The code is as follows:

```
ul {
    list-style-type: none;
    padding-left: 1em;
    margin: 0;
}
```

The list-style-type declaration removes bullets when a list is displayed. The padding-left declaration indents the list items 1em.

❸ Add an `li` selector to the stylesheet.

While the `ul` selector deals with the list as a whole, the `li` selector defines the formatting for each individual item in the list. The rule code is shown below:

```
li {
   background-image:
url('../images/square2c.png');
   background-repeat: no-
repeat;
   background-position: 0 .1em;
   padding-left: 1.25em;
   line-height: 140%;
}
```

The `background-image` declaration specifies the 12-x-12-pixel image file being used as a bullet, while the `background-position` declaration tells where to position it on the text line. The `padding-left` declaration indicates that the list item text should be indented 1.25em, the space the bullet image will occupy.

❹ Choose File⇨Save to save your stylesheet.

❺ View your new page look in your browser.

Open the HTML page in your browser to view the final results of the makeover.

The book's example file for this makeover is `makeover_05_03.html`.

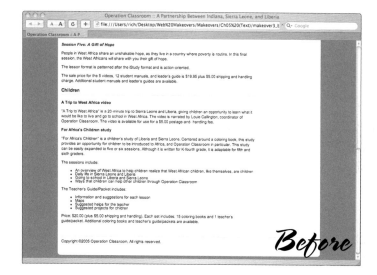

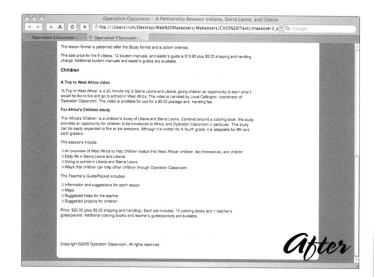

Before

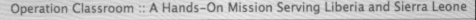

file:///Users/rich/Desktop/Web%20Makeovers/Working/Ch05/makeover2_after/index.html

om :: A H...

OPERATION CLASSROOM
A partnership between Indiana, Sierra Leone, and Liberia

HOME **PROGRAMS** **SHIPPING** **SUPPLIES** **VOLUNTEER** **RESOURCES** **ABOUT**

Home / Programs / Schools / Trip Reports

Field Trip Reports

Shippi

Volunte

Speake

Gifts

Smith and Iota Return from Sierra Leone

(Filed March 21.) Field Director Charles Smith and Chief Assistant Frank Iota recently had visited the Operation Classroom secondary schools in rural Sierra Leone. Over a two week span, they had a chance to visit over 16 schools, participate in their instruction, and even have a chance to play an occasional soccer game with the students. Read the full trip report »

Chip Stephens Unveils New Liberian Education Strategy

After

(Filed January 11.) Vice President Chip "Chippy" Stephens was in Monrovia, Liberia in January to unveil a new

6

IMAGE
MAKEOVERS

mage is everything. At least that's what a popular camera company used to tout in its ad campaigns. Although, in the Web world, images are definitely not everything, they are gosh darn important. Images are an integral part of any effective visual page design.

This chapter shows you four makeovers to help you use images better on your Web site. You start out by creating an image rollover. Next, now that everybody and his brother owns a digital camera, using photos on your site is easier than ever. However, the rectangular view you capture in your photo may not be the best way to show the image. Therefore, I walk you through the process of cropping your image to make it fit better into your visual design.

As you continue, you look at two techniques for displaying multiple pictures on a page. First, you discover the process of "thumbnailing" images and displaying them in a grid on a page. After that, you explore how to display said thumbnail images in a nifty gallery. Finally, I'll show you a makeover that enables you to overlay full-size images on a page.

Creating an Image Rollover

Rollovers are one of the most common ways to make a page instantly more interactive. Here's a makeover that enables you to add a rollover to your site in about the time it takes you to brew a cup of coffee.

① Determine which design elements on your Web page could benefit from an image rollover.

Navigation features, such as the icons you see in the upper right of the Web page here in the margin, are a natural.

② In Photoshop, create a button or set of buttons that you'll use for the normal, or "off," state.

The exact type of button style and shape depends on your page design. Save each image with an `_off` suffix as part of the filename.

If you're following along with the book examples, use the following four images that I came up with: `book_off.gif`, `song_off.gif`, `power_off.gif`, and `author_off.gif`.

③ Create a companion button or set of buttons for the "on" state of the rollover.

The image should be the same size as its companion but should be visually distinct to simulate a "highlight" effect. Save each image with an `_on` suffix as part of the filename.

For the book example, use the following images: `book_on.gif`, `song_on.gif`, `power_on.gif`, and `author_on.gif`.

④ In your Web page editor of choice, open the HTML file to which you'd like to add the rollover.

If you're following along with the book example, use the `makeover_06_01.html` file. (I use Dreamweaver here.)

⑤ If you're using Dreamweaver, click the Design button in the Document toolbar.

⑥ Position the cursor where you want to insert the image.

For the book example, click the image placeholder marked `book`.

⑦ If you don't already have an image placeholder in place, choose (in Dreamweaver, at least) Insert⇨Image from the menu. Alternatively, if you have an image placeholder (as in the book example), double-click the placeholder.

The Select Image Source dialog box appears. Navigate to the image you wish to insert, select it, and then click Choose (on a Mac) or OK (in Windows).

For the first book example, locate the `images/book_off.gif` file.

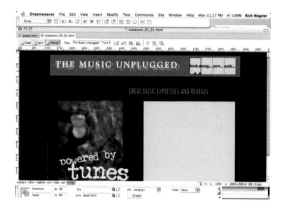

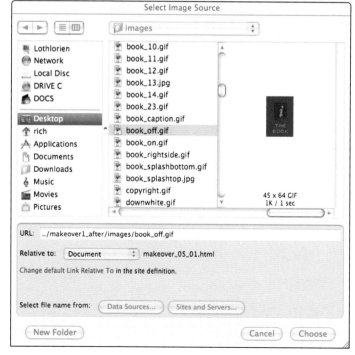

Creating an Image Rollover *(continued)*

The Image Tag Accessibility Attributes dialog box appears next.

⑧ In the Image Tag Accessibility Attributes dialog box, enter a label in the Alternate Text box and click OK.

The alternate text is important if the visitor's browser can't display graphics.

⑨ Enter a descriptive name for the `img` **element.**

In Dreamweaver, you enter a name in the Properties palette.

For the book example, enter `book`.

⑩ Repeat Steps 6–9 for each of the remaining images in your button set.

For the book example, add the following images in place of the placeholders: `images/song_off.gif`, `images/power_off.gif`, and `images/author_off.gif`.

⑪ If you're using Dreamweaver, click the Split button in the Document toolbar.

When you do so, you enter Split view, displaying both Design and Code panes of the document.

⑫ Insert a `script` **element inside the document head.**

In the Code pane, add the following code inside the `head` element:

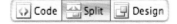

```
<script type="text/javascript"
language="Javascript"
charset="utf-8">
</script>
```

⑬ Add JavaScript code to the `script` element.

The code you add first checks to ensure browser compatibility. Next, it defines an "on" and "off" variable for code for each rollover image you plan to use. Here's what the code looks like:

```
if (document.images)
{rollovers=1};
if (rollovers)  {
      var book_on   = new
Image(); book_on.src =
'images/book_on.gif';
var book_off   = new Image();
      book_off.src =
'images/book_off.gif';
      }
```

Replace the `book_on` and `book_off` text with the names that match your images.

If you are working with the book example, enter all of the code as shown to the right.

⑭ Add (even more) JavaScript code to the `script` element.

You use two JavaScript functions to script your rollovers. The `rolloverOn()` function is called when a mouse hovers over a rollover image. The `rolloverOff()` function is triggered when a mouse moves off a rollover image.

Enter this code inside the `script` element:

```
function rolloverOn( imgName )
      {if ( rollovers ) {
document[imgName].src = eval(
imgName + "_on.src" );}}

function rolloverOff( imgName )
      {if ( rollovers ) {
document[imgName].src = eval(
imgName + "_off.src" );}}
```

Creating an Image Rollover *(continued)*

⑮ In the Design pane — assuming you're using Dreamweaver — select the first rollover image.

When you select the image in Design view, the img element is also selected in Code view.

⑯ In the Code pane, add handlers for the onMouseOver **and** onMouseOut **events inside the** img **panes.**

Add the following code to the img element. *Note:* Replace the book string inside the parentheses with the name parameter of the img element:

```
onmouseover="rolloverOn('book')"
onmouseout="rolloverOff('book')"
```

⑰ Repeat Step 14 for each rollover image.

⑱ Choose File⇨Save to save your HTML file.

Save it before you look at your handiwork.

⑲ View your new page look in your browser.

Press F12 in Dreamweaver to test out your rollovers in the default browser.

Cropping Images to Shed the Useless Stuff

"More isn't always better, Linus. Sometimes it's just more."

That quote from the film *Sabrina* is a perfect way to think about this next makeover: Images are great on your Web page, but include only the portions of the image that enhance your overall visual design. When you include an entire image — particularly if it's a digital photo — you usually include stuff that is useless and distracting. In other words, sometimes it's just more.

Here's a makeover that shows you how to crop and reshape an image — such as the one you see here to the right — to complement your Web page.

❶ Open the HTML file that contains the image you want to crop.

If you're using Dreamweaver, choose File⇨ Open.

   If you're working with the examples I put together, open the `makeover_06_02.html` file.

   If you're not already in Design view, click the Design button on the Document toolbar.

❷ Determine the best shape for the image and its approximate size.

When you look at the image as part of the page, explore whether its current shape and size are ideal for the page design. Consider possible changes to make your image flow seamlessly with other parts of your page.

Cropping Images to Shed the Useless Stuff *(continued)*

For example, in the book example, I've determined that a "widescreen" rectangle actually works better with my page design and takes up less real estate than the current box shape.

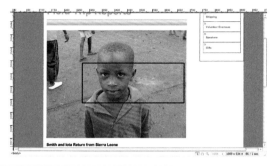

③ Determine the unnecessary parts of the image you are going to crop.

After you know the approximate shape and size of the image, determine the part of the image that should be included.

Rich's Take: Although you can make a final cropping decision while you are in Photoshop, you'll often find it helpful to eyeball the changes when you are looking at the image on the Web page itself.

When you've got a general idea what you want to accomplish, fire up Photoshop.

④ In Photoshop, open the image you want to crop.

Choose File➪Open.

Be sure to choose File➪Save As first and save the file under a new name, such as by adding _cropped to the filename. This enables you to make sure you can go back to your original image if you need to.

⑤ Choose the Crop tool from the Tools palette.

No need to worry about settings here — the Crop tool is easy to use.

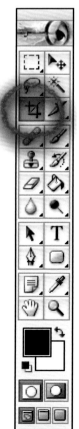

6 **With the Crop tool, draw the crop area.**

Use the Crop tool to select the portion of the image you wish to keep.

You can click and drag any side to adjust the dimensions of the cropped area.

7 **Press Enter to apply the crop.**

The cropped portion of the image is removed.

8 **If needed, resize the image to match your page design needs.**

Choose Image⇨Image Size to call up the Image Size dialog box. Adjust the dimensions and then click OK to carry out the image resizing.

If you're working with the book example, enter 555 in the Width box.

9 **Choose Filters⇨Sharpen⇨ Unsharp Mask.**

The Unsharp Mask filter helps enhance the quality of an image you resized.

10 **In the Unsharp Mask dialog box, set the Amount field to 100 percent, the Radius to 1.0 pixels, and the Threshold to 0, and then click OK.**

These settings give your resized image a crisper look.

The cropped image is now ready to go.

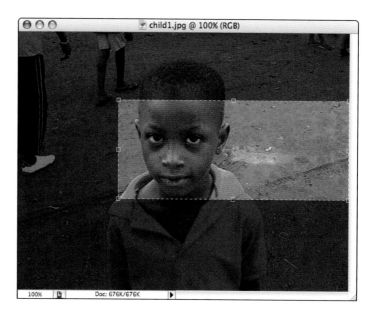

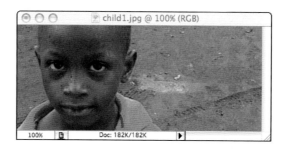

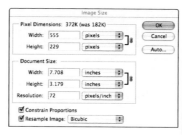

Cropping Images to Shed the Useless Stuff *(continued)*

⑪ Choose File➪Save to save changes.

Be sure the image is safely stowed away before manipulating it further.

⑫ Back in Dreamweaver, select the image in Design view and clear any previous Width and Height values from the Properties palette.

Clearing your previous settings ensures that the image isn't resized to the dimensions of the original image.

⑬ Choose File➪Save.

The idea here is to now save changes to your HTML file.

⑭ View your newly cropped image in your browser.

Press F12 in Dreamweaver to check out your cropped image inside your Web page.

Thumbnailing Images

When you have a gallery of images that you'd like to display on your Web site, the last thing you want to do is add a bunch of full-sized pictures to a single page. Your visitors will get impatient and then irked that they have to wait for a massively large page to download before viewing. (Even nice pages, like what you see here to the right, won't be appreciated if your Web visitor won't hang around long enough for it to load.)

Instead, a much better solution is to use small thumbnail images. These small images are quick to download and can be linked to their full-sized counterparts if the user wants to see the large-sized picture.

For this makeover, you create the thumbnail images in Photoshop and then add them to a table grid inside a Web page by using Dreamweaver.

Note: This makeover requires the use of a Photoshop Action, which is available for download at the Web site associated with this book. Before starting Photoshop, copy `Makeover Thumbnails.atn` into the Photoshop Actions folder in your Photoshop application's Presets subfolder.

➊ Copy all the images you wish to thumbnail into a separate folder (such as a `gallery` subfolder in your `images` subfolder).

Placing all of the images in a central location not only makes it easier to keep organized, but it also enables you to perform a batch operation to process all of the thumbnails at once.

Thumbnailing Images *(continued)*

For the book example, the original images are already located in the `makeover_06_03\images\gallery` (Windows) or `makeover_06_03:images:gallery` (Mac) subfolder.

② In Photoshop, choose Window⇨ Actions to display the Actions palette and then click the arrow button.

The Actions pop-up menu makes a special guest appearance.

③ Choose the Load Actions command from the pop-up menu.

The Load dialog box appears.

④ Select the `Makeover Thumbnails.atn` file from the list and click OK.

The Makeover Thumbnails Actions are now ready to use inside Photoshop.

⑤ Close any open files and then choose File⇨Automate⇨Batch.

The Batch dialog box opens. This nifty, time-saving feature enables you to perform a Photoshop Action on all files matching a certain criterion.

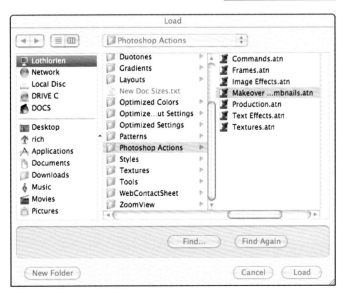

⑥ Choose Makeover Thumbnails.atn **from the Set drop-down list.**

The Makeover Thumbnails action set is a group of two actions I put together specifically for this book.

⑦ In the Action drop-down list, choose Thumbnailer.

The Thumbnailer Action resizes the existing file to 80 pixels wide, keeping the height in proper proportion.

⑧ In the Source drop-down list, choose Folder.

"Source" here means the "raw stuff" you want to sic your action on.

⑨ Click the Choose button right underneath the Source drop-down list.

Doing so calls up the Choose a Batch Folder dialog box.

⑩ In the Choose a Batch Folder dialog box that appears, select the folder you placed all of the images in back in Step 1; then click OK.

You're brought back to the Batch dialog box.

⑪ Choose Folder from the Batch dialog box's Destination drop-down list.

You get to choose where your images go after you've worked them over.

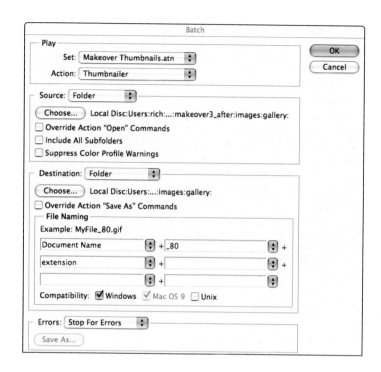

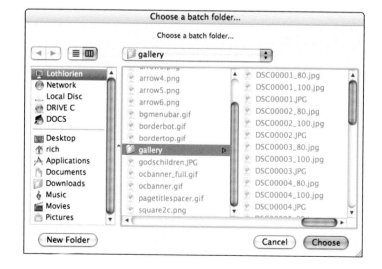

Thumbnailing Images *(continued)*

⓬ Click the Choose button right underneath the Destination drop-down list.

Use the Choose a Batch Folder dialog box to select the target folder for the thumbnails.

Rich's Take: I recommend placing them in the same folder as the originals to make managing the images easier.

⓭ In the File Naming section of the Batch dialog box, select Document Name from the first drop-down list, choose (or type) _80 in the second drop-down list, and select Extension from the third drop-down list.

This section defines the naming conventions for your thumbnails. These instructions tell Photoshop to add a _80 suffix to the original filename, indicating 80 pixels in width.

⓮ At the bottom of the Batch dialog box, choose Stop for Errors from the Errors drop-down list.

By selecting this option, Photoshop will inform you of any errors encountered during the process and will stop the batch process.

⓯ Click OK.

You'll notice Photoshop acting like it has a mind of its own, opening each image in the source folder and downsizing it.

Note: When a JPG file is processed, a JPEG Options dialog box will appear, asking you to specify the image quality. For thumbnails, I recommend keeping the rating at 5. Click OK after you've set the options to continue processing.

⓰ In Dreamweaver, open the Thumbnail Template page and then save it under a new filename.

Choose File⇨Open from the menu and open `thumbnails_starter.html`. You can find the `thumbnails_starter.html` file on the Web site associated with this book.

The Dreamweaver starter page for thumbnails features a 1 x 3 table grid. However, I've enhanced that original page to include a 3 x 3 grid.

Open this starter file and then choose File⇨Save As and give your HTML file a new name.

If you're following along with the book example, use the `makeover_06_04.html` file. This features an empty 3 x 3 grid inside the now familiar OC template.

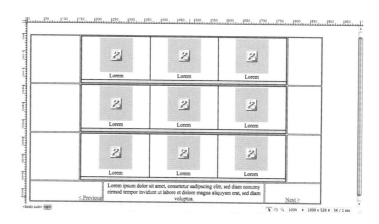

⓱ Select the placeholder image in the top-left corner of the grid and then enter the filename of your first thumbnail in the Src box in the Properties palette that appears.

You can click the Browse for File button if you would like to select the image from a dialog box.

⓲ Link the thumbnail image to the original file by entering the file-name in the Link box in the Properties palette.

Linking the images is optional, but it does give the viewer an opportunity to see the full-scale photo.

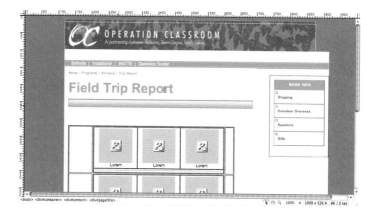

Thumbnailing Images *(continued)*

⑲ Add a text label under the thumbnail image.

Here's a good chance to provide a descriptive caption for your thumbnail.

⑳ Repeat Steps 17–19 for each of the remaining thumbnail images in the grid.

㉑ Update the greeked text as appropriate for your Web page.

Greeked text is a series of somewhat non-sense sentences that serves as placeholder text.

㉒ If you have nine or fewer thumbnails, remove the Previous and Next links at the bottom of the page. Otherwise, add URLs for these links in the Properties palette.

㉓ Choose File⇨Save.

Doing so saves all changes to your HTML file.

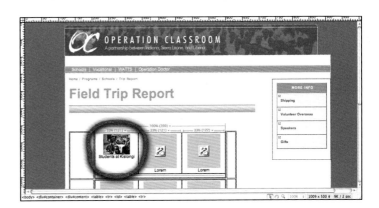

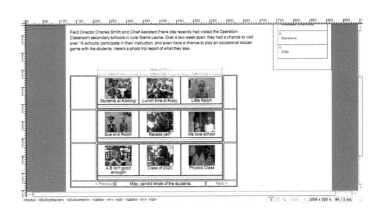

㉔ Repeat Steps 16–23 for each set of nine thumbnails in your group.

㉕ Open your starting HTML file in your browser to see the results.

Clicking any of the thumbnails displays the full-size companion.

Displaying Multiple Images with an Image Scroller

Thumbnails are often displayed in a fixed table (as shown in the previous makeover), but the downside is the amount of space that they take up on a page when you have several to show.

Here's a makeover that enables you to display multiple thumbnails inside an image scroller that visitors can control with a mouse.

Note: Like the previous makeover, this makeover walks you through the process of creating thumbnail images in Photoshop. The process here is virtually the same, except the thumbnails are 100 pixels wide rather than 80.

In addition, this makeover requires a Photoshop Action to be used — it's available for download from the Web site associated with this book. (In fact, it's the same Action I used in the previous makeover.) Before starting Photoshop, copy `Makeover Thumbnails.atn` into your Photoshop Actions folder in your Photoshop application's Presets subfolder.

❶ Copy all of the images you wish to thumbnail into a separate folder (such as a `gallery` subfolder in your `images` subfolder).

Placing all of the images in a central location not only makes it easier to keep organized, but it also enables you to perform a batch operation to process all of the thumbnails at once.

Note: If you performed the previous makeover and have 80-pixel thumbnail images in the folder, be sure to move them temporarily while you perform this thumbnailing process. (After you're done, you can move them back.)

For the book example, the original images are already located in the `makeover_06_04\images\gallery` (Windows) or `makeover_06_04:images:gallery` (Mac) subfolder.

❷ In Photoshop, close any open files and then choose File⇨Automate⇨Batch.

The Batch dialog box opens.

Note: If you did not previously load the Makeover Thumbnails Action set into Photoshop, follow Steps 2–4 in the previous makeover before continuing.

❸ Choose `Makeover Thumbnails.atn` from the Set drop-down list.

The Makeover Thumbnails Action set is a group of two actions I put together specifically for this chapter.

❹ From the Action drop-down list, choose Scroller Thumbnail.

The Scroller Thumbnail action resizes the existing images to 100 pixels wide, keeping the height in proper proportion.

❺ In the Source list, choose Folder.

Again, "Source" here means the "raw stuff" you want to sic your action on.

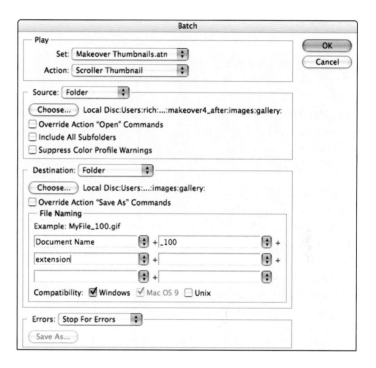

Displaying Multiple Images with an Image Scroller *(continued)*

⑥ Click the Choose button right underneath the Source drop-down list.

The Choose a Batch Folder dialog box appears.

⑦ Use the Choose a Batch Folder dialog box to select the folder you placed all of the images in back in Step 1 and then click Choose.

You're brought back to the Batch dialog box.

⑧ Choose Folder from the Batch dialog box's Destination drop-down list.

The idea here is to find a place to keep all your transformed images.

⑨ Click the Choose button right underneath the Destination drop-down list.

Use the Choose a Batch Folder dialog box to select the target folder for the thumbnails.

Rich's Take: I recommend placing them in the same folder as the originals to make managing the images easier.

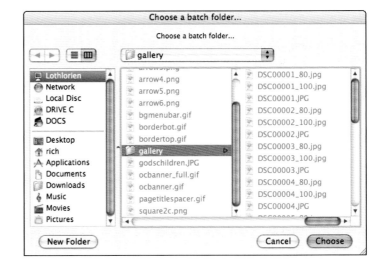

⑩ In the File Naming section of the Batch dialog box, select Document Name from the first drop-down list, select (or type) _100 in the second drop-down list, and select Extension from the third drop-down list.

This section defines the naming conventions for your thumbnails. These instructions tell Photoshop to add a _100 suffix to the original filenames, indicating 100 pixels in width.

⑪ At the bottom of the Batch dialog box, choose Stop for Errors from the Errors drop-down list.

By selecting this option, Photoshop will inform you of any errors it encounters during the process and will stop the batch process.

⑫ Click OK.

You'll notice Photoshop acting like it has a mind of its own, opening each image in the source folder and downsizing it.

Note: When a JPG file is processed, a JPEG Options dialog box will appear, asking you to specify the image quality. For thumbnails, I recommend keeping the rating at 5. Click OK after you've set the options to continue processing.

⑬ Copy the `gallerystyle.css` **and** `motiongallery.js` **files into your css folder.**

These two files control the image scroller. You can find them for download on the Web site associated with this book.

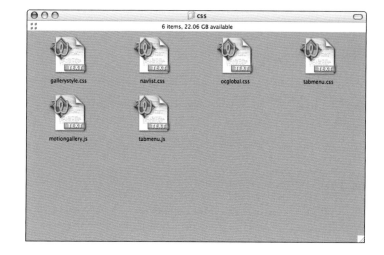

Displaying Multiple Images with an Image Scroller *(continued)*

⑭ In Dreamweaver, open the Web page to which you wish to add the image scroller.

Choose File➪Open and select the file in the Open dialog box.

If you are working with the book example, choose `makeover_06_04.html`.

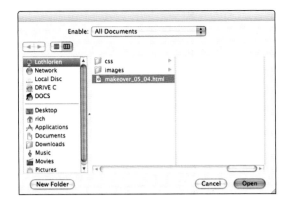

⑮ Click the Code button in the Document toolbar to view the HTML code.

⑯ In the document head, add link and script elements referencing an external CSS stylesheet and JavaScript library file.

Enter the following code to connect your file with the image scroller support files:

```
<link rel="stylesheet"
rev="stylesheet"
href="css/gallerystyle.css"
type="text/css" media="screen"
charset="utf-8" />
<script
src="css/motiongallery.js"
type="text/javascript"
language="Javascript1.2"
charset="utf-8">
/*******************
***************
* CMotion Image Gallery- (c)
Dynamic Drive DHTML code library
(www.dynamicdrive.com)
* Visit http://www.dynamicDrive.
com for hundreds of DHTML scripts
* This notice must stay intact
for legal use
*********************************
**************/
</script>
```

Rich's Take: You can go to www.dynamicDrive.com to check for any updates to the image gallery.

⑰ Choose the location in the document body where you want to place the image scroller and then add its container code.

Here's the code you need to add:

```
<div id="motioncontainer"
style="position:relative;width:40
0px;height:80px;overflow:hidden;m
argin-left:90px;">
<div id="motiongallery"
style="position:absolute;left:0;t
op:0;white-space: nowrap;">
<nobr id="trueContainer">
</nobr>
</div>
</div>
```

Adjust the width of the `motioncontainer` div based on your page design needs.

⑱ Inside the `trueContainer` `nobr` element, add code for the first thumbnail you wish to include in the image scroller.

Enter the following `a` and `img` elements, substituting the `img src` value for the image file you are including and then adding the linked full-size image as the parameter inside the `enlargeimage` function:

```
<a href="javascript:enlargeim-
age('images/gallery/DSC00003.JPG'
)"><img
src="images/gallery/DSC00003_100.
JPG" border=1></a>
```

Displaying Multiple Images with an Image Scroller *(continued)*

⑲ Repeat Step 18 for each thumbnail image in your gallery.

The more, the merrier.

⑳ Just under the image scroller container, add explanatory text letting visitors know how to work the control.

Add the following HTML code:

```
<p style="text-align:center;font-
size:80%;">Scroll the gallery by
using your mouse. Then click on
an image to enlarge it.</p>
```

㉑ Save changes to your HTML file.

Choose File⇨Save in Dreamweaver.

㉒ View your image scroller in your browser.

Press F12 in Dreamweaver to test out your image scroller in the default browser.

Check out the image gallery functionality. Hover the mouse pointer over the thumbnail images and then move the pointer to the right side of the gallery. As you do so, the image gallery begins to scroll automatically to the right, showing the images that were "off screen." Then, when you stop scrolling the mouse, the gallery does the same. You can scroll back to the left simply by moving the mouse leftward.

When a user clicks a thumbnail image, the full-sized window appears, but this time in a pop-up window.

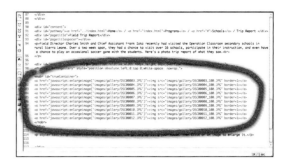

Before

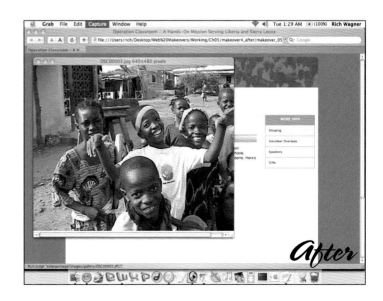

After

Displaying a "Lightbox" Overlay Image

While the previous makeover provided a great way to display thumbnail images, the downside was that the larger image opened in a second browser window. Although it's functional, that solution isn't necessarily the most aesthetically pleasing.

Here's a makeover that offers a great alternative: overlaying the full-size image on top of the existing Web page.

Note: Before you begin this makeover, you need to download `lightbox.css`, `lightbox.js`, `overlay.png`, and `loading.gif` from Web site associated with this book. (These resources are the components of the Lightbox JS script, written by Lokesh Dhakar, www. huddletogether.com/projects/ lightbox.) Copy `lightbox.css` and `lightbox.js` into your `css` subfolder for your Web site and place the two image files into your images subfolder.

❶ Open an HTML file that contains thumbnails that you wish to link to an overlayed image.

Choose File⇨Open from the menu.

If you're working through the book examples, open `makeover_06_05.html`.

If you're using Dreamweaver and you're not already in Code view, click the Code button on the Document toolbar.

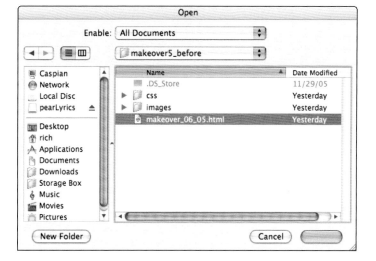

Displaying a "Lightbox" Overlay Image *(continued)*

② **Add a** `link` **element into your document head to connect the** `lightbox.css` **stylesheet with your Web page.**

The following code should be added anywhere inside your `head` element:

```
<link rel="stylesheet"
rev="stylesheet" href="css/
gallerystyle.css" type="text/css"
media="screen" charset="utf-8" />
```

③ **Add a** `script` **element into your document head to include** `lightbox.js`.

The `lightbox.js` file contains the scripting logic for performing the image overlay. Here's the code to add:

```
<script src="css/lightbox.js"
type="text/javascript"
language="Javascript1.2"
charset="utf-8"></script>
```

④ **Scroll down to the code that displays your thumbnail images.**

A standard thumbnail image, such as the ones you've worked with in earlier makeovers in this chapter, is usually an `img` element housed inside an accompanying `a` element. The `a` element links the smaller thumbnail image to a full-sized version using the `href` attribute.

If you're following along with the book example or are working with the image scroller from the previous makeover, look for the `trueContainer nobr` element.

⑤ In the a element associated with each thumbnail img, add a standard URL reference to the full-sized image.

If you're following along with the book example or are working with the image scroller from the last makeover, you'll need to replace the javascript:enlargeimage() references with standard URL references.

⑥ Add a rel="lightbox" attribute to the a element of each thumbnail image.

The rel attribute is used by the script code inside lightbox.js.

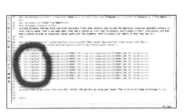

⑦ Save changes to your HTML file.

Choosing File⇨Save from your menu will do the trick.

⑧ Check out the new image overlay in your browser.

If you're using Dreamweaver, press F12 to display the page in the default browser.

To test it out, click the thumbnail image of your choice. The full-sized image is then loaded and displayed on top of the original page. A gray, semi-transparent overlay darkens the original page.

Click the full-sized image to close the overlay image and return to the original page.

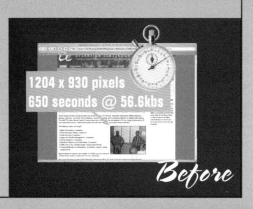

1204 x 930 pixels
650 seconds @ 56.6kbs

Before

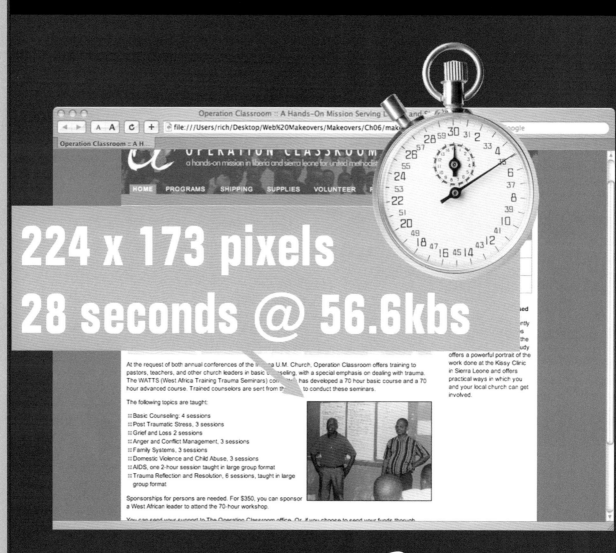

224 x 173 pixels
28 seconds @ 56.6kbs

After

7 IMAGE PERFORMANCE MAKEOVERS

Making over your Web site involves more than just transforming your site into something visually attractive and easy to navigate. You also need to consider how responsive your Web pages are to your visitors, particularly those who use a 56 Kbps dial-up connection. In fact, for users with modem access, the effectiveness of your Web site is based as much on its overall speed as it is on your visual design.

In cyberspace, text is cheap. You can say a lot without taking up much bandwidth. Instead, when it comes to sluggish Web page performance, the number-one culprit is nearly always the overall file size of the images you place on the page. Often, a single image is not the problem, but rather a set of unoptimized images needlessly slows down the performance of your entire Web site.

In this chapter, you explore how to optimize your images. You begin by using Photoshop to resize your images manually rather than letting the browser do it for you. A second makeover shows you how to shrink an image's file size without adversely affecting its overall quality. Finally, you discover how to use JavaScript to preload images you use in your site to avoid unnecessary delays.

Resizing Images Yourself

Many Web site–building tools, such as Dreamweaver or FrontPage, allow you to place any image onto your HTML page and resize it to the size that fits your needs. This resizing technique may be easy to do, but I recommend avoiding this option. The software doesn't resize the actual image; it simply tweaks the height and width properties in the associated `img` tag. As a result, you can be unaware of your image's "weight problem." A visitor to the original Operation Classroom Web site, for example, had to download a 1204 x 930-pixel image (weighing over 3MB!) on its home page, even though it only displayed the image in a modest 383 x 214-pixel rectangular box. (You can see this particular chubby Web page here on the right — note how long it takes for the page to load in a browser!)

Here's a makeover to ensure the images you place on your HTML page are sized for speed.

① Find an image on your site that needs shrinking.

If you're working through the examples in the book, you'll be working with the `teaching.jpg` image, which is referenced by the `makeover_07_01.html` file.

❷ Open the image in Photoshop.

Choose File⇨Open from the menu to display the Open dialog box. Then navigate to your image (`teaching.jpg` if you're following this book's example), select it, and click Open.

❸ Choose File⇨Save As and rename the original file.

If you don't intend to modify the HTML page that the image is already added to, then you need to name the smaller image you are creating with the same name. If so, rename the original file to a new name in case you want to use it in the future.

If you're working with the book example, name the file `teaching_large.jpg`.

If your file is a JPG file, you'll see the JPEG Options dialog box. Keep the default options for now and click OK.

❹ Choose Image⇨Duplicate.

Be sure you work from a copy so you can keep your original intact.

Enter a name for the image in the Duplicate Image dialog box.

❺ Choose Image⇨Size from the menu.

The Image Size dialog box is displayed.

❻ Enter 224 in the Width box.

The Height box is automatically recalculated to 173. Keep these settings and click OK to resize.

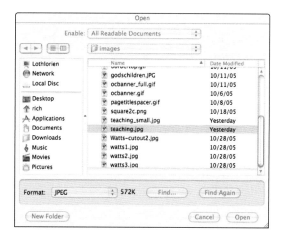

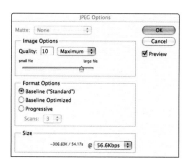

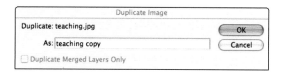

Chapter 7: Image Performance Makeovers

Resizing Images Yourself *(continued)*

The image is now sized to smaller dimensions, eliminating the need for you to let the browser do the resizing.

⑦ Choose File⇨Save For Web.

The Save For Web dialog box appears.

⑧ In the Save For Web dialog box, choose JPEG in the file type drop-down list.

Keep the rest of the defaults for now. You focus on optimizing these kinds of settings in the next makeover.

⑨ Click Save to continue.

The Save Optimized As dialog box makes an appearance.

⑩ Enter the name of the original image file in the Save Optimized As dialog box and click Save to continue.

If you are overwriting an existing file, you'll be asked to confirm the overwrite.

For the book example, enter **teaching.jpg**.

⑪ View the results of your makeover by opening the HTML page in your browser.

While the page will look the same as before, it will now load far more quickly. On your local computer, you may not notice much of a difference. But when you upload your image file to your Web site, your dial-up visitors will notice a major difference.

In the book example, for instance, the image goes from 572K to 40K — over 14 times smaller!

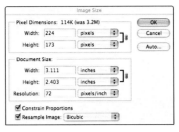

Reducing Your Image's File Size, Not Its Quality

Life is a game of give and take. This expression may or may not be valid for the real world, but it certainly applies to images on the Web. Any Web image has different qualities associated with it, such as dimension (width and height), "weight" (file size), number of colors, and file type (JPG, GIF, or PNG). The challenge is finding the right "give and take" among all these factors that allows you to display great-looking images with a minimum of download time.

This makeover shows you how to optimize your images in Photoshop.

❶ Find an image on your site that needs optimization.

If you're working through the examples in this book, you'll be working with the `teaching.jpg` image, which is referenced by the `makeover_07_02.html` file.

❷ Open your image in Photoshop.

Choose File⇨Open from the menu to display the Open dialog box.

❸ Choose File⇨Save As to rename the original file.

Before continuing, you should save your original, unoptimized image under a different name.

If you are working through the examples in the book, name the file `teaching_114.jpg`.

Click Save to continue. If you are working with a JPG image, you'll see the JPEG Options dialog box appear next.

Reducing Your Image's File Size, Not Its Quality *(continued)*

④ Keep the default options in the JPEG Options dialog box and click OK.

Now that your original file is taken care of, you are ready to get on with the makeover.

⑤ Choose Image⇨Duplicate.

Working off a copy of the image prevents you from overwriting the original.

Enter a name for the image in the Duplicate Image dialog box. For the book example, **teaching** will do just fine.

⑥ Choose File⇨Save For Web.

The Save For Web dialog box appears.

⑦ Select the appropriate optimized file format from the format drop-down list.

The type of image format you use will vary according to your need. If you're working with a photo, use JPEG (or PNG-24). If you're working with a graphic that has text and a smaller number of colors, or if you need part of the image to be transparent, GIF or PNG-8 may be possible options.

If you are trying to decide which optimized format is most appropriate for your needs, try various formats. For each one, look at the quality of the image in the preview window and the optimized file size shown in the lower-left corner of the dialog box. Experiment with various settings until you have a quality and size combination you are satisfied with.

⑧ For JPEG images, lower the Quality slider to the smallest possible number that still maintains sufficient image quality.

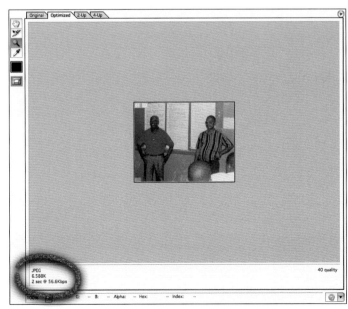

Remember my talk about "give and take"? Here's where that comes into play. As you move below 60, you'll slowly begin to see a loss in image quality. The image loss may be barely noticeable for a while, but after you get below 40, the loss will be increasingly apparent.

Keep an eye on the image preview window and file size while you select the right quality level.

If you're working with the book example, select 40. This value is a good tradeoff between image quality and image size.

⑨ Click Save to continue.

The Save Optimized As dialog box is displayed.

⑩ Enter the name of the original image file in the Save Optimized As dialog box and click Save.

For the book example, type **teaching.jpg**.

If you are overwriting an existing file, you'll be asked to confirm the overwrite.

If you don't type the appropriate file extension, Photoshop will append the appropriate extension onto the end of your filename.

⑪ View the makeover by opening the HTML page in your browser.

As with the first makeover in this chapter, you won't notice any significant visual differences. But the page will load much more quickly after you upload the updated, optimized image to your Web site.

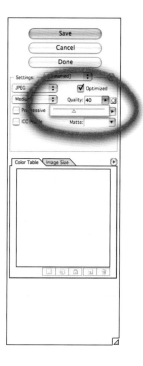

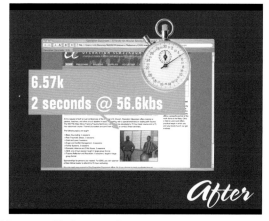

Preloading Images

When you are using a rollover (see Chapter 6) or another image effect that makes use of multiple images, you don't want its performance marred by constantly downloading the image that the effect calls for at a given point in time.

By using JavaScript, you can preload any images you plan to use with a rollover or other image effect. When you preload an image, JavaScript loads the requested images as the document head is being retrieved and stores them in the browser cache. Then, as the image is requested by the visitor, the newly cached image is displayed instantaneously.

Follow the steps below to make over your image rollovers by preloading your images.

❶ Open an HTML page whose images you wish to preload.

In Dreamweaver, choose File➪Open.

If you're working with the book examples, open the makeover_07_03.html file.

❷ View the HTML code for the page.

In Dreamweaver, click the Code button on the Document toolbar.

❸ In the document head, add a `script` element.

The `script` element will contain your image preloader code.

❹ Add a code line that tests to ensure that the browser supports rollovers.

All modern browsers support the `document.images` object, but you still want to cover your bases for possible really, really old browsers out there. Enter the following code line in the script element:

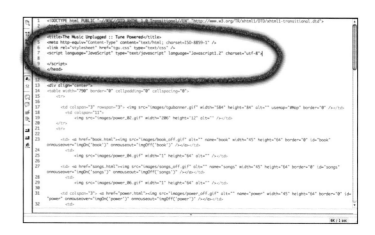

```
if (document.images) {
doRollovers=1 };
```

⑤ Create an Image object for both the "on" and "off" versions of the image.

A rollover has two states, depending on whether the mouse is hovering over it. You want to define JavaScript Image objects for each of these instances.

For each "on" and "off" image, create a new instance of the Image object and then assign a src value to it. Here's an example:

```
var book_on  = new Image();
book_on.src =
'images/book_on.gif';
```

When the code is executed, the browser loads the image from the specified URL and stores it in its cache.

If you're working with the book examples, you'll want to define eight object instances, as shown to the right.

⑥ Save changes to your HTML page.

Choose File➪Save from the Dreamweaver menu.

⑦ In Dreamweaver, choose File➪ Preview in Browser and then choose the desired browser in which to view the performance improvements.

The rollover image that you originally added back in Chapter 6 will now show improved performance as you mouse over the images.

When all of the files are coming from your local computer, the time saved will be insignificant. However, when you upload the updated files to your Web server, you'll see a definite speed increase in your rollovers.

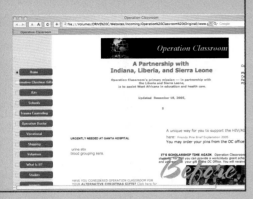

8

HOME PAGE MAKEOVERS

Home sweet home. Not only should that old adage be your aim in the real world, but it also should reflect the care and attention you give to your Web site's home page. After all, if visitors to your site don't like what they see on the first page they encounter, they'll rapidly click their browsers' Back buttons and never come back.

This chapter is all about making over your home page to provide both first-time visitors and regulars — two distinct audiences — the information that they are looking for or the path to get to it quickly. You begin by looking at how to "message" your home page for all types of people coming to your site. You then do some housecleaning and throw out everything that doesn't communicate that message or gets in the way of communicating it. Next, you explore ways to transform your home page from online "brochureware" to something that feels alive. Finally, you put a wrap on the chapter by exploring how to add a splash introduction to your site.

Messaging Your Home Page

A well-designed home page is never mis-taken for a patchwork quilt — a hodgepodge of information all woven together onto a single page. Instead, you need to design your home page by purposefully considering exactly who is coming to your Web site and what kind of information they are looking for. Your job as a Web site designer is to con-nect the two seamlessly.

Here's a makeover that guides you through the process of messaging your home page.

As you work your way through your home page, I show you the steps I take to create the home page for the Operation Classroom (OC) Web site, seen here to the right.

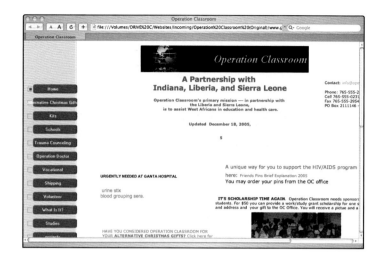

① On a piece of paper, jot down the various types of visitors coming to your site.

Before being able to message your home page, you first need to know whom you're trying to communicate with. Write down the various *personas* (different types of peo-ple) who come to your site.

For the OC site I am working with, I sketched out six distinct personas, as shown on the right.

② Cluster the personas into groups.

You'll often group together first-time visi-tors and regulars, but you may also have additional groups to define.

Indiana-based volunteers helping with shipments
People interested in volunteering overseas
People/groups desiring speakers and other resource info
Partners getting latest info on OC

First-time visitors who want to learn about organization.

Responders to current fund-raising campaign

For the OC site, I have three distinct groupings — first-timers and regulars are constant, while the special group varies according to current fund-raising campaigns.

③ Determine the goals you have for each group.

For the OC site, I want to easily provide first-timers with the information they need in order to both understand the organization and recognize the opportunities it has for involvement. For the regulars, the site should provide the information that they need in order to better partner with OC. And, for the special campaign group, I want to provide one-click access to a page designed for the current fund-raising campaign.

④ Prioritize the visitor groups to determine the amount of focus you should give each one on your home page.

Decide which groups should get primary attention or whether you should give them equal attention.

Regulars
- Indiana-based volunteers helping with shipments
- People interested in volunteering overseas
- People/groups desiring speakers and other resource info
- Partners getting latest info on OC

First-timers
- First-time visitors who want to learn about organization

Special
- Responders to current fund-raising campaign

Messaging Your Home Page *(continued)*

For the OC site, regulars generate the majority of traffic, so they get slightly more attention than anyone else. However, first-timers will get much attention as well.

⑤ Develop specific messages or content targeting each visitor group.

As you do so, decide whether any common messages or content can effectively serve multiple groups.

For example, with the OC site, a "get involved" message works equally well with regulars and first-timers.

After you refine your messages and content, you are ready to put them on your home page.

⑥ In your Web page editor of choice, open the `homepage_template.html` **file.**

The `homepage_template.html` file is available for download from the Web site associated with this book. This three-columned Web page (when used in conjunction with `global.css`, a stylesheet that controls the site's formatting) is a good starter template for you.

⑦ Save the template under a new filename.

In Dreamweaver, you choose File⇨Save As and enter a new filename, such as `index. html`, in the space provided. Click Save.

Both ~ Get involved and make a difference

Regulars ~ Latest news from the field, info on next shipping, and workteam schedules

First-timers ~ info on organization (Who We Are)

8 Customize the Web page and stylesheet to meet your design needs.

The `homepage_template.html` file is based on the OC demo site discussed throughout this book, so you will need to tweak the colors and images to meet your site needs.

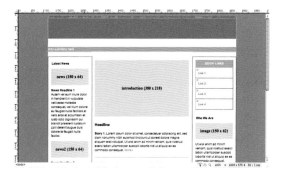

You want to populate the `mainMenu` and `submenu` `div` elements with links for your site. You also want to be sure to use the `global.css` file, which is available for download from the book's Web site.

9 If you're using Dreamweaver, click the Design button on the Document toolbar.

The HTML file is displayed in Design view.

Other Web page editors have other ways of calling up their versions of Design view. Please check your documentation.

10 Add primary message content in the center section (the `content div` element).

The content and message you most want to communicate should be placed in the `content div` in the center column.

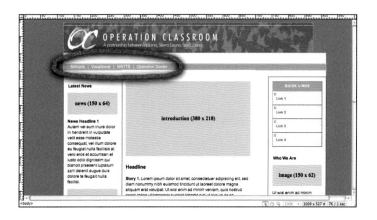

For example, with the OC site, I designed a graphic, headline, and short paragraph blurbs all focused on the "get involved" message. (The small 48-x-48 graphic icons beside each story are a nice touch, if I do say so myself.)

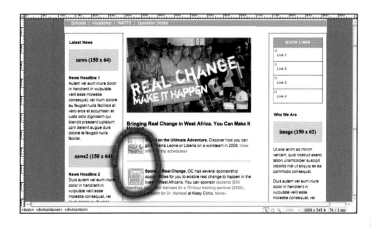

Messaging Your Home Page *(continued)*

⑪ Populate the `navlist` vertical menu with links to your most popular pages.

Highlight popular links in the `navlist`. For example, in the OC page, the organization found that "regulars" requested four pages most.

By adding this quick-links list, you can offer one-click access to regular visitors for the pages most used, while still providing the full top-level menu for first-timers.

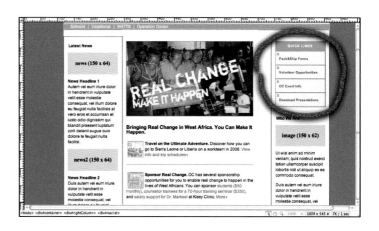

⑫ Add secondary content below the `navlist`.

I target first-time visitors here by adding a "Who We Are" section. Here's a chance to briefly tell people about the organization, providing a link to the About Us page for full details.

⑬ Add any special content above the `navlist`.

Although you don't have room to add any substantive text above the `navlist` menu, the top-right corner is a good location for adding a small graphical link to notify people of a sale or campaign.

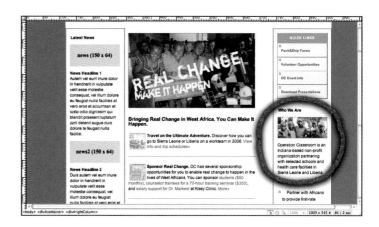

For example, to direct the third visitor group of the OC site — people coming to the site to respond to a special "Project 2006" campaign — I added a graphical link.

Rich's Take: Be careful adding a graphic that might compete with the overall focus of the page. For example, with the OC site, I used a faded tan color with minimal text to ensure that a visitor's focus remains on the Real Change content in the middle of the page.

⑭ Save your changes.

In Dreamweaver, choose File⇨Save.

⑮ Preview your home page.

You add the "Latest News" section in the next makeover, so check out the state of the home page transformation so far.

To display your home page, click the Preview/Debug in Browser button on the Document toolbar. Next, select the browser of your choice from the pop-up menu.

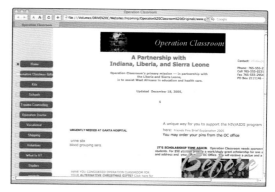

Author Confidential

The Home Page Quartet

The exact needs of your home page depend on the nature of your Web site. However, nearly all Web sites should adhere to the "Home Page Quartet":

The handshake. Your home page should be like a warm, helpful handshake, providing quick, obliging access to the information that first-time guests and long-time regulars are searching for.

The neighborhood bakery. Your home page should offer fresh and timely content, like your local baker, not like the day-old-bread store.

The kitchen sink. The content of your home page should never be "kitchen sinked" — in other words, putting everything on your page *including* the kitchen sink. Don't clutter the page with unnecessary extras.

The eye candy. Your home page should be "eye candy," the best-looking page on your site, to grab the attention of people coming to your site.

Making Your Home Page Feel Alive

The kiss of death for a Web site is having it referred to as "static" or "brochureware." If you aren't careful, even effective sites, such as the one you see here to the right, can start to feel stale to visitors — and if that happens, they'll never feel a need to return to your site, as helpful and effective as it may be. As a result, you need to make your Web site feel "alive" to people when they visit so that they will bookmark it and check back regularly.

There are many ways to transform your site, but adding a news section is one of the best ways. Follow the steps below to do just that.

① Carve out a section of your home page to devote to news.

If you performed the previous makeover, you already have the left column ready-set for news. I assume you are working with that tri-column layout for the rest of this makeover.

② In your Web page editor of choice, open your home page.

In Dreamweaver, choose File⇨Open and select your file from the Open dialog box.

③ Click the Design button on the Document toolbar.

The HTML file is displayed in Design view.

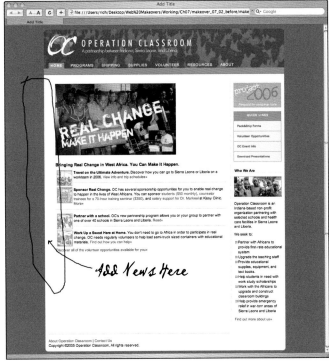

④ Add one or more news stories to the Latest News section of the page.

Keep the news stories relatively brief (preferably 50 words). If the full story is more than 100 words, display the first 50 words and then create a link to a secondary news page that has the full details.

Rich's Take: Be sure to date your story and add a descriptive title to it.

At the bottom of the news section, add a link to a news story archives page. This enables people who've not visited your site recently to get up to date on the events and stories that you've been discussing.

⑤ Replace the news image placeholder with a 150-x-64-pixel image to accompany the story.

If you have any photos or other images that help describe the news story, add the image reference in the `Src` box of the Properties palette. If the Properties palette isn't visible, you can display it by choosing Window⇨ Properties from the Dreamweaver menu.

⑥ To highlight newly posted stories, add a "new" icon after the headline.

A "new" icon is a great way to enable regulars to quickly spot recently posted stories.

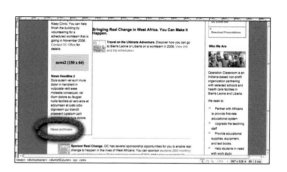

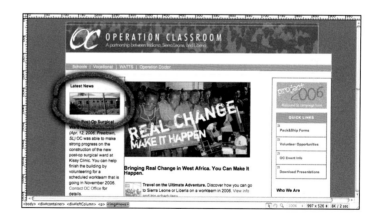

Making Your Home Page Feel Alive *(continued)*

In Dreamweaver, you choose Insert⇨ Image and then select the `new.gif` image, which is available for download from the Web site associated with this book. Click Choose to insert the image.

⑦ Save your changes.

In Dreamweaver, choose File⇨Save.

⑧ Preview your home page.

Press F12 in Dreamweaver to display your "fresh" home page in the default browser.

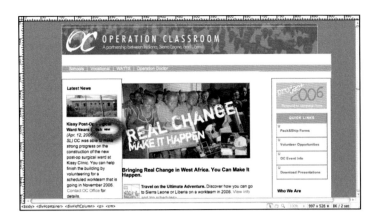

Adding a Splash Introduction

Sometimes you just want to make a "splash" — grabbing visitors' attention before you let them browse your site. Perhaps you aim to launch a new product line. Maybe your goal is simply to introduce who you are. In the Web world, you can do this through an introduction or splash page.

Many Web introductions are created in Macromedia Flash. If you know how to work with Flash, you can use it to create professional-looking introductions. However, here's an alternative for you to consider — a makeover that uses normal HTML and JavaScript to create an effective splash introduction for your site.

Rich's Take: Splash introductions can be an effective and acceptable way to communicate with your site visitors. However, be warned that some people just get annoyed by them. Therefore, if you are going to add one to your site, make sure you follow two rules: (1) provide an easy way for visitors to skip the splash intro (such as a Skip link), and (2) only show the intro to the visitors the first time they visit the site, not each visit.

Here's how to add this makeover.

① Prepare the text and images you would like to include in your splash introduction.

A splash introduction consists of two or more separate screens (or pages) that are displayed automatically, much like a slide presentation.

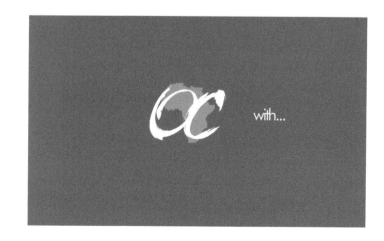

Adding a Splash Introduction *(continued)*

Your first step is to gather the text and images you plan to use.

② Rename your home page file to `index2.html`.

The HTML file containing your splash introduction will effectively become your new home page. However, when the introduction finishes, it automatically redirects the browser to another page you specify, which will be your normal home page.

Use Finder or File Manager to rename your original home page.

③ Using your Web page editor of choice, open `intro_splash_template.html`.

The `intro_splash_template.html` can be found on the Web site associated with this book. (You can quickly customize this particular Web page to fit your particular needs.)

④ Save the file as `index.html`.

In Dreamweaver, choose File⇨Save As and enter `index.html` in the space provided. Click Save.

⑤ Click the Code button on the Document toolbar.

All of the customization for this makeover is done inside of the HTML code itself.

⑥ Adjust the `bgcolor` and `text` attributes of the document body to match the look of your site.

If you are following along with the book example, change the `bgcolor` attribute to #1D6963. You can leave the text color unchanged at #FFFFFF.

⑦ Inside the `script` **element, locate the** `var preloadimages` **definition.**

⑧ In the parentheses of `var preloadimages = new Array()`**, add the URLs that point to the images you want to include in your splash introduction.**

This code preloads the images to ensure a smooth introduction.

⑨ Adjust the `intervals` **variable assignment, if needed.**

The normal delay between each screen is two seconds. If you would like to speed up or slow down this setting, tweak the `var intervals` value assignment, which is measured in milliseconds.

⑩ Adjust the `target destination` **variable assignment, if needed.**

If your actual home page filename is `index2.html`, then skip this step. Otherwise, adjust the assignment to the URL of your home page.

⑪ Locate the `openingtag` **variable assignment and add any style or formatting HTML tags that you want to include.**

For example, if you want to use a `font` or `style` element to assign formatting to the entire splash introduction, add the opening tags inside the quotes.

Adding a Splash Introduction *(continued)*

For the book example, leave this as an empty string because the example uses all images and no text.

⑫ In the `closingtag` **variable assignment, enter the matching closing tag for each opening tag you used in the** `openingtag` **variable.**

For the book example, you can leave the `closingtag` variable unchanged.

⑬ Add content for each of the slides in the `splashmessage[]` **assignments.**

Inside the quotation marks, add text or HTML code to display the content for each screen of your splash introduction.

For the book example, enter the `img` element code as shown in the figure to the right.

Add or remove `splashmessage` array items based on the number of screens you want to include in your splash introduction.

If your real home page is named `index2.html`, then skip Step 14. Otherwise, continue on.

```
11  <layer id="splashcontainerns" width=450></layer>
12
13  <script type="text/javascript" language="Javascript1.2" charset="utf-8">
14
15  //Specify the URLs of the images to be used in the splash screen, if any.
16  //If none, empty out array (ie: preloadimages=new Array())
17  var preloadimages=new Array("images/splash1.gif","images/splash2.gif", "images/splash3.gif", "images/splash4.gif")
18  //Configure delay in milliseconds between each message (default: 2000, or 2 seconds)
19  var intervals=2000
20  //configure destination URL
21  var targetdestination="index2.html"
22
23  //Configure messages to be displayed
24  //   * Each splashmessage item is displayed as a seperate "page" in the intro
25  //   * openingtags and closingtags should contain any style or font tags that you
26  //     wish to apply to entire introduction
27  //   * If message contains apostrophe, use backslash then (ie: "I\'m fine")
28  var splashmessage=new Array()
29  var openingtags=''
30  splashmessage[0]='<img src="images/splash1.gif"> '
31  splashmessage[1]='<img src="images/splash2.gif"> '
32  splashmessage[2]='<img src="images/splash3.gif"> '
33  splashmessage[3]='<img src="images/splash4.gif"> '
34  var closingtags=''
35
36
37
38  <!-- Core splash scripting logic -->
39  <script src="css/splash.js" type="text/javascript" language="Javascript1.2" charset="utf-8"></script>
40

<body>                                                                              2K / 1 sec
```

⑭ Scroll down to the bottom of the page and adjust the `href` **attribute of the** `a` **element to match the URL of your home page.**

You need to set this link in case the visitor decides to skip your prized introduction and simply go to the normal home page.

⑮ Save your changes.

In Dreamweaver, choose File⇨Save.

⑯ Test your splash introduction.

Click the Preview/Debug in Browser button on the Document toolbar. Then click the desired browser from the list to test out your splash introduction.

One of the great advantages of this makeover is that the splash introduction only displays the first time a visitor comes to the site. Thereafter, the intro is bypassed, and the user is taken directly to the real home page. This logic is handled automatically for you inside of the `splash.js` file.

Before

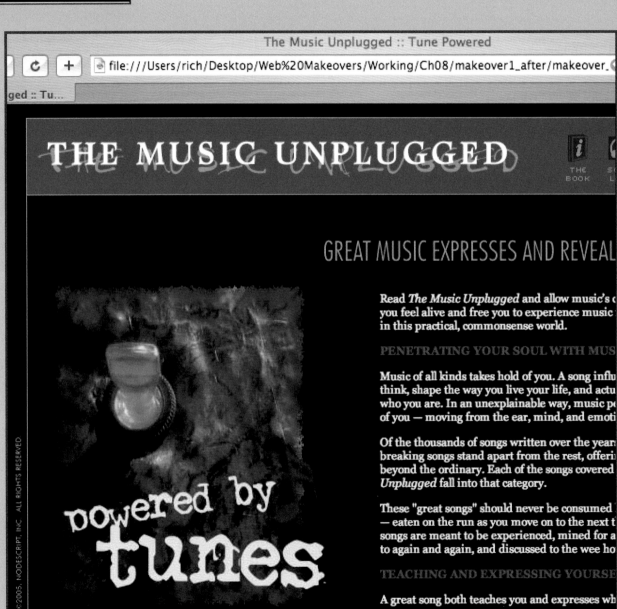

After

9 CONTENT MAKEOVERS

Read me! This is interesting stuff! Really! Care about me!

Though obviously overstated, these ideas are essentially the message you are trying to communicate to your Web site's visitors when they browse your content. We live in an attention-starved world in which we constantly flip the remote and surf the Web. In such an environment, you can't expect visitors to read your pages from start to finish like they do with a book, magazine, or brochure. In fact, you could write better than Hemingway, but it won't matter if you don't know how to write for the Web.

In this chapter, you explore how to transform the content of your Web site to better communicate with (and make it more readable for) your visitors. You begin by walking through a series of tips to change your content into Web-savvy text. Next, I show you how to place and label your links to make them more readable and effective. Finally, I walk you through two makeovers that provide an alternate print version of a Web page without the need to add a second page.

Writing Web-Savvy Text

Writing for the Web is not the same as writing for other media. The content may be the same, but the way in which people read it is far different. People rarely read word for word when they're Web surfing; instead, they scan and skim looking for specific bits and pieces of info. Your goal should be to have your Web site interact with the readers, keeping them engaged as they surf through your site.

The following makeover walks you through the process of transforming your page content from a print-centric model of blocks and blocks of text (see the page to the right) into Web-savvy text — content that is short, scannable, and to the point.

❶ Using your Web page editor of choice, open an HTML file that contains content you wish to make over.

In Dreamweaver, you choose File⇨Open to display the Open dialog box. Choose the file and click Open.

If you're following along with the book's example, open `makeover_09_01.html`.

❷ If you're using Dreamweaver, click the Design button in the Document toolbar.

You'll be editing the text, so you want to work in Design view.

Scan your site and look, in particular, for pages that

> ➤ Have long, dense paragraphs.

> ➤ Use little or no headings or subheadings.

> ➤ Use jargon or phrases that may not be recognized by first-time visitors to your Web site.

> ➤ Read like an impersonal owner's manual.

③ Read through your text and get rid of anything unnecessary.

On the Web, you'll usually find that less is more. Therefore, before doing any word-smithing on your page, you first should read through and get rid of text that is simply not needed.

In my example, I identified a brief, super-fluous anecdote at the end of my first paragraph that didn't help make the point I was trying to make. So I removed it.

④ Place your best stuff at the top of the page.

Lead with the most compelling information; never save it for the end, like you would if you were writing a novel.

Don't waste time and space with well-crafted prose introducing you or your topic, just get to the heart of the matter.

The original text in the book example saved the clincher line ("read this book") for the last line of the page. Instead, I moved that line up to the top to help "frame" the page and let people know why they should read this page.

⑤ Break up large sections of text into smaller paragraphs that are easier for readers to scan.

Take a pickaxe to any "Berlin walls" of text — long, intimidating paragraphs that are deadly to Web readers. Rephrase your prose with short, conversational chunks of text.

⑥ Add headings and subheadings to break up your content into man-ageable sections.

Headings and subheadings make it easy to scan a long article and get the gist of where it is taking you.

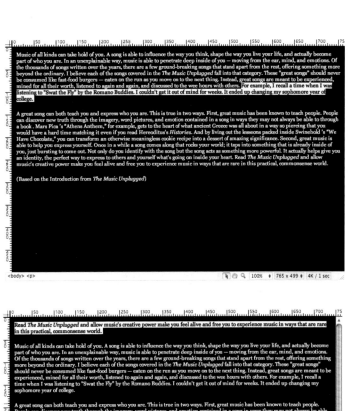

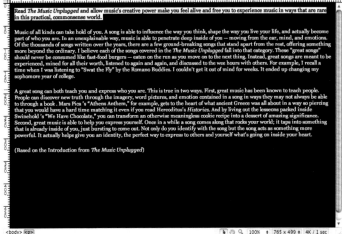

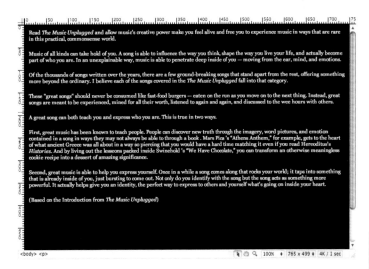

Writing Web-Savvy Text *(continued)*

In the book example, I added two sub-headings (using action-oriented and attention-grabbing words).

❼ Read through your text and convert any lists and series of words or phrases into bulleted lists.

The example text had a two-part paragraph set that lended itself to being reworked into a bulleted list. In converting to a list, I removed "First" and "Second" from the start of the paragraphs and boldfaced the first sentences.

I then decided to break the first list item into multiple paragraphs to separate the text even more.

❽ Throw out the jargon, acronyms, and fluff.

Remove any technical or insider jargon or acronyms that first-time visitors may be clueless about. Also, rephrase or delete obvious marketing fluff.

After you've made an initial pass, read through your content once again to examine how appropriate and relevant it is for a visitor who knows nothing about you or your Web site.

❾ Change "being" verbs into action verbs.

Transform passive verbs like *was, has been, is,* and *were* into verbs of action. Active sentence are far more compelling than passive ones.

❿ Make *you* the subject rather than using a third-person subject.

When you use *you* in your text, you engage visitors and draw them into your page. (Check out all the *yous* I added to the text in the Web page to the right.)

⓫ Identify link opportunities inside your page content.

A common saying is, "If you don't have links, you are not writing for the Web." Look for parts of your text that can be linked to other parts of your Web site or to other sites.

⑫ Date your content.

When visitors browse your Web site, you need to let them know when you wrote the content of a page. Without letting them know it, they have no idea whether the information is recent or several years old.

⑬ Save your changes in your HTML file.

As always, choose File➪Save to save your editing tweaks.

Press F12 to preview your Web-savvy text inside your default browser.

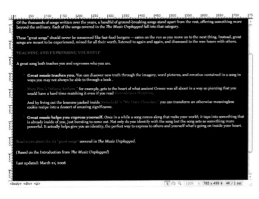

Creating Intuitive and Usable Links

If the Web is powered by links, then your Web site should make it easy for your visitors to "push the throttle" and click away.

Here's a makeover to help transform your existing — and probably not too obvious — text links (see the Web page to the right) into clickable text that is intuitive and natural for your visitors.

❶ Using your Web page editor of choice, open an HTML file whose textual links you'd like to modify.

In Dreamweaver, you choose File⇨Open from the menu. Choose the file of your choice and click Open.

Open `makeover_09_02.html` if you are working through the book examples.

❷ If you're using Dreamweaver, click the Design button in the Document toolbar.

Because you're working with the text, you'll find it easier to work in Design view.

❸ Reword your links so that the text intuitively lets the user know where they are heading and what they'll find when they get there.

"Click here" or "click me" are too vague and non-descriptive, so throw out any of these statements.

Use action verbs if possible.

For the book example, the "two week span" link was too vague, so I added a much more descriptive parenthetical comment, enabling the visitor to view the team's Web calendar. I also axed the "click here" links, rephrasing the links to start with active verbs and adding greater clarity by adding a fuller phrase to be part of the link.

❹ Optionally provide a visual indicator of the link.

For some links, you might find it helpful to include an arrow image or text arrow to indicate a link.

Rich's Take: You can use `&raquo;` to display the guillemet, the French quote mark (»). Or you can use double greater-than signs (>>).

⑤ Remove any underlining on text that is not linked.

On the Web, an underlined word screams, "Click me!" Underlining text for the sake of emphasis just confuses readers. Instead, use bold or italics.

⑥ Save your editing changes in your HTML file.

When you have finished, choose File⇨Save.

⑦ Test out your new links inside your browser.

Pressing F12 in Dreamweaver displays the page in the default browser.

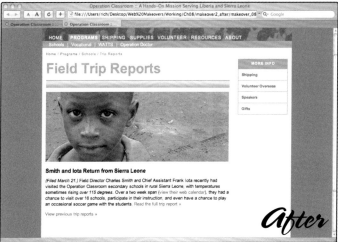

Adding an Alternate Print Version of Your Web Page

The visual design you developed for your Web site is oriented exclusively toward a great appearance and experience inside a browser. (The Web page to the right, for example, looks perfect in a browser, if I do say so myself.) However, you'll often find that the decisions you make for Web page design may not look so great when you print the page on paper. A fixed layout, for example, may look fabulous inside a browser, but the content on its right edge may be cut off when the page is printed. In addition, colored text that works in your design on screen may be hard to read when printed on an ink jet printer.

Therefore, if you have articles, white papers, or other pages that readers may wish to print, consider the following makeover.

Note: For this makeover, I assume you are using the `div`-based page layout design discussed in Chapter 1. If your layout differs, apply the same principles to your specific context.

❶ In your Web page editor of choice, open the CSS stylesheet that contains your document styles.

In Dreamweaver, you choose File⇨Open from the menu. Then, in the Open dialog box, choose the file of your choice and click Open.

If you are working with the book example, open `ocglobal.css`.

❷ Save the stylesheet under a new name.

You want to create a modified version of the stylesheet customized for print output, so you should save an original version of the stylesheet to be safe.

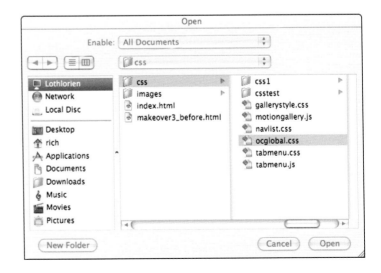

In Dreamweaver, choose File⟶Save As and give the stylesheet a new name.

For the book example, save it as `ocprint.css`.

③ Change your background color to white.

A printed version looks best as black text on white, so remove any colored formatting you may have.

For the book example, modify the HTML code by changing the `body` selector's `background-color` style to #FFFFFF.

④ Still working within the `body` selector code, change the font to a font size suitable for normal printing.

Although a smaller font may produce optimal results for a Web context, you want to use something larger for printing.

For the book example, I changed the `body` selector's font styling to:

```
font: 85%/1em Arial, Helvetica,
sans-serif;
```

Rich's Take: If you use sans serif fonts, you may wish to use them in the printable version for consistency. Alternatively, you may wish to switch to a serif font, as this type of typeface is often the most readable on printed materials.

Here's the modified body selector based on Steps 3 and 4:

```
body {
        background-color:#FFFFFF;
/* White background */
        margin-top:0px;
        font: 85%/1em Arial,
Helvetica, sans-serif; /*
Enlarged font for printing */
}
```

```
1
2   /**
3    * General HTML Body Styling
4    * --------------------------
5    */
6   b
7       background-color:#FFFFFF; /* White background */
8       margin-top:0px;
9       font: 85%/1em Arial, Helvetica, sans-serif; /* Enlarged font for printing */
10  }
11
12  a { text-decoration: none }
13
14  a {
15      text-decoration: none;
16          color : #1D6963;
17  }
18
19  a:hover {
20          color: #CC7E55;
21
22  }
23
24  img { display:none; } /* Hide for printing */
25
```

3K / 1 sec

Adding an Alternate Print Version
of Your Web Page *(continued)*

⑤ If you have a fixed-width layout, change the width of the #container selector to a percentage-based layout.

A fixed width has certain visual design advantages for the Web, but these strengths quickly turn to disadvantages when it comes to printing. (Chief among such disadvantages is that content can get cut off from the right edge of the page — not something that is going to prompt a lot of reader loyalty.)

Instead, if you are using the #container div layout model, as defined in Chapter 1, change the #container's width to 100%.

Here's the updated code:

```
#container {
      width:100%; /* Percentage-
based layout */
      margin: 0 auto;
      background-color:#FFFFFF;
}
```

⑥ Hide all of the page elements you don't want printed by changing their style to display:none.

The display:none rule causes the browser to ignore any element to which it is assigned. You want to set this rule for several parts of the Web page, including the menu, banner graphic, right column, and footer.

If you are using the div-based layout and the related navigational menu (discussed in Chapters 2 and 3), you want to apply the display:none rule by replacing existing selectors with the following:

```
#header, #pathway, #pagetitle-
spacer, #rightColumn,
#footer, #topBorder,
#bottomBorder, #mainMenu,
#mainMenu a,
#submenu, #submenu a{
      display:none; /* Hide for
printing */
}
```

```
48
49
50    #container {
51        width:100%; /* Percentage-based layout */
52        margin: 0 auto;
53        background-color:#FFFFFF;

55
56    #header, #pathway, #pagetitlespacer, #rightColumn,
57    #footer, #topBorder, #bottomBorder,  #mainMenu, #mainMenu a,
58    #submenu, #submenu a{
59        display:none; /* Hide for printing */
60    }
61
62    #content {
63        padding: 1em;
64        /*  margin-right: 175px; */  /* Disabled for printing */
65        background-color:#FFFFFF;
66        min-height: 550px;
67    }
68
69    #pagetitle {
70        font-size: 3.25em;
71        font-weight: bold;
```

3K / 1 sec

Note: The `#mainMenu`, `#submenu`, and their related `a` selectors are defined in the `tabmenu.css` file, but you don't need to make any changes to the original file. The changes you make in this makeover will override the original settings. (Yes, there's a reason that the "C" in "CSS" stands for "cascading.")

You may wish to apply this rule to your image elements as well:

```
img { display:none; } /* Hide for
printing */
```

❼ Disable or remove any margin or padding settings that are based on the original screen layout.

With the Chapter 2 `div`-based layout, the `#content div` element has a margin-right rule that you need to comment out or delete:

```
#content {
      padding: 1em;
      /* margin-right: 175px; */
/* Disabled for printing */
      background-color:#FFFFFF;
      min-height: 550px;
}
```

❽ Remove any additional style settings that are inappropriate for print-only versions of the page.

If you're following the `div`-based layout used throughout the book, you want to remove the `ul` selector and replace the style rules of the `li` selector to match the basic formatting of the `p` element. (See the figure on the right.)

❾ Save your changes to your new print-oriented stylesheet.

Choose File⤵Save in Dreamweaver.

Your stylesheet for printing is now ready to go.

```
24  img { display:none; } /* Hide for printing */
25
26  p { line-height
27
28  li { line-height: 1.35em; }  /* Delete custom settings, make consistent with p element */
29
30  h1
31
32        font: 185%/1em Arial, Helvetica, sans-serif;
33        font-size: 1.95em;
34        font-weight: bold;
35  }
36
37  hr {
38        border: none;
39        border-top: 1px solid #cccccc;
40        height : 3px;
41        width : 100%;
42  }
43
44  /**
45   * Basic DIV Elements
46   * -----------------------
```

`3K / 1 sec`

Adding an Alternate Print Version of Your Web Page *(continued)*

⑩ In your Web page editor of choice, open an HTML file in which you'd like to add an alternative print version.

In Dreamweaver, choose File⇨Open from the menu to display the Open dialog box. Choose the file and click Open.

If you're following along with the book example, open the `makeover_09_03.html` file.

⑪ If you're using Dreamweaver, click the Design button in the Document toolbar.

You first must add a Print button, which is usually easier to do in Design view.

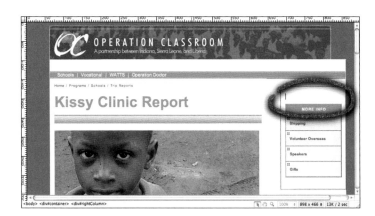

⑫ Position your cursor where you wish to add the Print button.

The top of the right column is a great place to add it.

⑬ Choose Insert⇨Image.

The Select Image Source dialog box appears. Browse and select `btn_print.gif` (located in the `images` subfolder under the `makeover_09_03` directory) or another image you'd like to use.

Click Choose (Mac) or OK (Windows).

The Image Tag Accessibility Attributes dialog box now makes an appearance.

⑭ Add "Print page" as the alternate text in the Image Tag Accessibility Attributes dialog box.

The alternate text shows up when a browser can't display the button image.

Click OK to continue.

⑮ With the image selected, enter `JavaScript:showPrintVersion()` in the Link box of the Properties palette.

A JavaScript routine named `showPrintVersion()` is going to be called when the image is clicked. This routine does all the hard work to get the page reformatted for printing.

⑯ Click the Code button in the Document toolbar.

You'll want to work now with the underlying HTML code for this makeover, so you should move to Code view.

⑰ Link your print-oriented stylesheet to the HTML file by adding a `link` element to the document head.

Because of the cascading nature of CSS, place the new `link` element *before* your other `link` elements that include external stylesheets. Here's the code for the new `link` element:

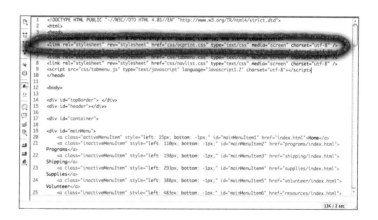

```
<link rel="stylesheet"
rev="stylesheet"
href="css/ocprint.css"
type="text/css" media="screen"
charset="utf-8" />
```

⑱ Add a new `script` element to the document head.

The `script` element will contain JavaScript code used to display the alternate print version of the document.

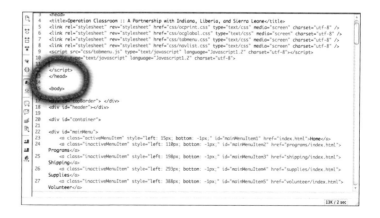

Adding an Alternate Print Version
of Your Web Page *(continued)*

⑲ Add the JavaScript code needed to switch active stylesheets and open the print version in a new window.

The code to enter is shown on the right. (You can save typing by finding it in the `makeover_09_03_after.html` file.)

The `showPrintVersion()` function is called when the Print button is clicked. It opens the same document in a new window and calls the `toggleStylesheet()` function, which enables the print stylesheet and disables the others.

Rich's Take: Decide whether you want the Print dialog to automatically display when the window is loaded. If you'd like this capability, uncomment the `wHnd.print()` line.

⑳ Save the changes you made to your HTML file.

In Dreamweaver, choose File⇨Save.

㉑ Preview your new alternate print version feature in your browser.

Pressing F12 in Dreamweaver takes you there.

Before

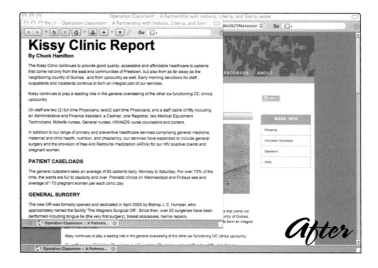

After

Adding an Alternate Print Version of Your Web Page, Technique II

The preceding makeover showed you how to display an alternate print version of your Web page in a separate window. Users can then print out that new version on their printers.

Here's a second technique to add an alternate print version of your Web page. This option is easier to implement, but has a possible downside: It sends the alternate version directly to the printer without informing the user that a different layout is being used.

❶ Prepare your print-oriented stylesheet.

If you worked through the preceding makeover, you already have one created. If not, follow Steps 1–9 of the previous makeover before continuing.

❷ In your Web page editor of choice, open an HTML file to which you'd like to add an alternative print version.

In Dreamweaver, choose File⇨Open from the menu to display the Open dialog box. Choose the file and click Open.

If you're working with the book examples, open the `makeover_09_04.html` file.

❸ Click the Code button in the Document toolbar.

You don't need to make any visual changes to the page; instead, you just add a single line of code.

④ Link your print-oriented stylesheet into the HTML file by adding a `link` element to the document head.

Here's the code for the new `link` element:

```
<link rel="stylesheet"
rev="stylesheet"
href="css/ocprint.css"
type="text/css" media="print"
charset="utf-8" />
```

Note the `media="print"` attribute. The `print` value tells the browser to use the associated stylesheet when it prints the page.

⑤ Save the changes you made to your HTML file.

In Dreamweaver, choose File⭢Save.

⑥ Print your Web page from inside your browser.

Press F12 in Dreamweaver to display the HTML file in your default browser. Then choose File⭢Print (or File⭢Print Preview). The page generated for the printer uses your print-oriented stylesheet. The figure to the right shows the printable page using Safari's Print Preview function.

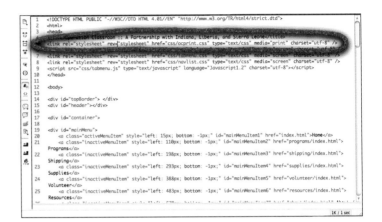

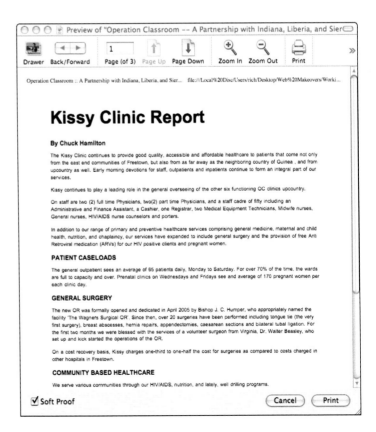

Adding a Subject and Message to a mailto Link

A `mailto` link is a handy way to make it easy for site visitors to send you an e-mail. When people click the link, a new message window appears in their e-mail software. The `mailto` link automatically adds the e-mail address you supply as the recipient of the message. However, the visitor still needs to add a subject and body text to the message.

Here's a makeover that allows you to set up the message subject and even the body text automatically.

Note: This `mailto` makeover works in all modern browsers, but may not always perform as expected in legacy browsers.

❶ Open the HTML file that contains the `mailto` link you'd like to enhance.

Choose File⇨Open in Dreamweaver or your HTML editor.

If you'd like to work through an example I came up with, open `makeover_09_05.html`.

If you aren't already in Design view, click the Design button on the Document toolbar.

❷ Place the text cursor inside the `mailto` link that you'd like to make over.

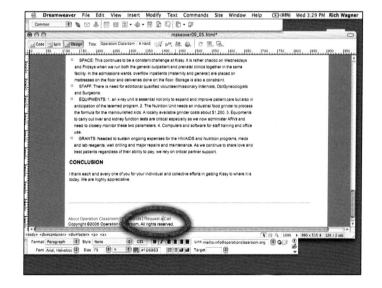

If you're working with the book example, scroll down to the footer and click anywhere on the `Request a Call` link.

The Link box in the Properties palette displays the current `mailto` URL.

Adding a Subject and Message to a mailto Link *(continued)*

❸ Add a message subject by appending `?subject=` `SubjectText` **to your** `mailto` **URL (where** `SubjectText` **is any text string of your choice).**

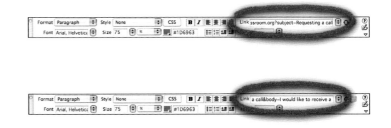

For the book example, add

```
?subject=Requesting a call.
```

If you'd like to add text to the message itself, proceed to Step 4. Otherwise, skip the next step.

❹ Add body text by appending `&body=BodyText` **to your** `mailto` **URL (where** `BodyText` **is the actual default text of your message).**

If you're working through the book example, add

```
&body=I would like to receive a
call at your earliest conven-
ience. Please call me at
[****Enter phone number here****]
```

❺ Save your changes.

Choose File⇨Save before doing anything else.

❻ Test your makeover.

Open the page in your browser. Using Dreamweaver, you can choose File⇨ Preview in Browser and then choose your desired browser.

Click your made-over `mailto` link to display the new e-mail message window.

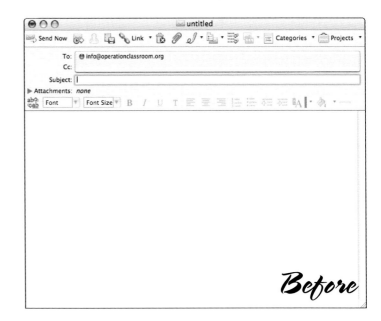

Before

After

mailto parameters

You can now add far more than just a recipient's e-mail address to `mailto` URLs. Here's a list of different options.

> `?subject=`*Text*: Subject of message
>
> `&body=`*Text*: Body text of message

`&cc=`*EmailAddress*: Carbon copy recipient

`&bcc=` *EmailAddress*: Blind carbon copy recipient

You can mix and match these various parameters, but the maximum number of characters allowed in the complete `mailto` URL is 256.

digitalwalk: the magazine

subscribe

BILL TO:

First Name   Charley
Last Name   Wongriller
Company
Address
☐ Ship to same address
City   Lantern Waste
State   WY
Zip/Postal Code   29100
Phone
Email Address   charley.com
☑ I wish to receive a weekly email newsletter
* indicates required field
Reset   Submit

Before

digitalwalk: the magazine

subscr

BILL TO:

First Name   Charley
Last Name   Wongriller
Company
Address   *** Problem - Field is required
☐ Ship to same address
City   Cair Paravel
State   WY
Zip/Postal Code   29100
Phone
Email Address   charley.com   *** Problem - Invalid email address
☑ I wish to receive the weekly email newsletter

Gray background indicates required field

After

Reset

10

FORM MAKEOVERS

"Form follows function. . . . has been misunderstood," architect Frank Lloyd Wright once remarked. "Form and function should be one, joined in a spiritual union." If Wright is right, then nowhere is this axiom more appropriate in the Web world than in building forms. Forms, after all, are perhaps the most function-oriented feature of any Web site: They aren't designed to be sexy; they're designed to collect data — so much so that they typically conjure up images of accountants, not artists or designers.

In this chapter, I focus on makeovers that improve both the function and the appearance of your Web forms. I start out by showing how to make your forms smarter by both validating the data input by your site visitors and customizing the tab order of your form. From there, I concentrate on the look of the form itself. As I do so, I explore how to use CSS to transform a generic form into something that complements your site's look and feel. Finally, I wrap up the chapter by showing you how to replace the standard HTML buttons with graphical buttons you make yourself in Photoshop.

You can follow along in the chapter by applying the makeovers to your own forms. However, feel free to work with the HTML files and images that I highlight in this chapter. For each of the four makeovers, I start with the `subscribe_before.html` file found at the Web site associated with this book.

Validating Your Forms

Forms like the one you see here on the right are only as useful to you as the quality of the data you can gather from them. One of the ways in which you can better ensure you are getting the data you want is to validate the data *before* the site visitor submits the form to the Web server for processing.

Form validation, however, can either be helpful or downright annoying for the person filling out the form. His or her reaction all depends on how you implement the logic. Good validation informs visitors of a problem and gently guides them to its source, but doesn't pester them in the process.

To perform this makeover, you need to add JavaScript code to your HTML file. Here's how you'd use that code to add form validation to your form without annoying your visitors.

Before you begin, take a moment to download the `formvalidate.js` file from the book's Web site and copy into your `css` subfolder.

❶ Open an HTML file that contains a form you wish to validate.

If you are using the example files I've come up with, open `makeover_01_01.html`.

Note: In my example, I perform four different types of validation: required fields (simply ensuring there's some text in the field) and special checks for state, zip code, and e-mail fields.

❷ View the HTML code of the file.

In Dreamweaver, you get to Code view by clicking the Code button in the Document toolbar.

Form validation is all done by JavaScript, so you need to work with the HTML source code to perform this makeover.

In the book example, scroll down to the form named `subform`. Notice the table inside the form: The first column contains the labels, the second column provides the field elements, and the final column contains empty tab cells that I use to contain any feedback I give to the user.

❸ Add a `script` element to the document head to reference the `formvalidate.js` source file.

The form validation routines you call are general-purpose and can be used with any HTML form. Therefore, rather than add these routines inside this file, I place them in a separate `.js` source file called `formvalidate.js` to make them easier to reuse.

Reference the file by adding the following code in your document head:

```
<script
src="css/formvalidate.js"
type="text/javascript" language=
"JavaScript1.2" charset="utf-8">
</script>
```

Validating Your Forms *(continued)*

❹ Add an onchange **event handler for each of the input fields you wish to validate.**

The onchange attribute triggers when the user changes the value in the field and then leaves the field. This event proves ideal for performing validity checks on each field before the form is submitted.

The onchange event will call a JavaScript routine I defined in the formvalidate.js file using the following: checkRequired(this, "string"). You need to pass two bits of information to the function: this (which references the element calling the routine) and a string identifying the HTML element that houses any messages you need to communicate to the user concerning the current field.

For the book example, add the following onchange handler to the fname input element definition:

```
onchange="checkRequired( this,
'fnameErrDisplay' );"
```

Note: I am using a simple naming convention for the string value: the associated id of the input element followed by ErrDisplay. (I identify the fnameErrDisplay element in Step 5.)

Add the same code for the lname, address, and city fields, updating the value of the ErrDisplay handler to correspond with the name of the associated element.

The state, zcode, and email elements each have unique handlers, which are routines defined in the formvalidate. js file: checkState(this, "stateErrDisplay") for the state element; checkZipCode(this, "zcodeErrDisplay") for the zcode field; and checkEmail(this,

```
151  <div id="content">
152  <form id="subform" name="subform" method="post" onsubmit="return validateAllFields()" action="dosomething.cgi">
153  <table width="651" border="0" cellpadding="1" cellspacing="1" summary="Billing address table">
154  <tr>
155      <td width="116" height="29" align="left"><span>Bill To:</span></td>
156      <td width="242" align="left"></td>
157
158  <tr>
159      <td width="116" align="right"><label for="fname">First Name</label></td>
160      <td width="283" align="left"><input name="fname" type="text" class="inputboxreq" id="fname" size="" onchange=
     "checkRequired(this, 'fnameErrDisplay');"/></td>
162      <td width="242" align="left"> </td>
163  </tr>
164  <tr>
165      <td width="116" align="right"><label for="lname">Last Name</label></td>
166      <td width="283" align="left"><input name="lname" type="text" class="inputboxreq" id="lname" size="" onchange=
     "checkRequired(this, 'lnameErrDisplay');"/></td>
167      <td width="242" align="left"> </td>
168  </tr>
169  <tr>
170      <td width="116" align="right"><label for="company">Company</label></td>
171      <td width="283" align="left"><input name="company" type="text" class="inputbox" id="company" size="30" /></td>
172      <td width="242" align="left"> </td>
173
174  <tr>
175      <td width="116" align="right"><label for="address">Address</label></td>
176      <td width="283" align="left"><input name="address" type="text" class="inputboxreq" id="address" size="" onchange=
     "checkRequired(this, 'addressErrDisplay');"/></td>
177      <td width="242" align="left"> </td>
```

"emailErrDisplay") for the email element.

You don't need to validate the company and address2 fields, so you don't need to worry about adding handlers to them.

⑤ Add id attributes to each of the elements that will contain your field-level feedback.

Rather than popping up alert message boxes for each problem, a more user-friendly solution is to provide a place beside each field that can display problems when the user moves off of a field.

Use an empty table cell or other element that can serve as the location for this information.

Give each element a unique id attribute that you can reference. This id value is referenced in the onchange event defined in Step 3.

If you are following along with the example, begin by adding id="fnameErr Display" to the empty td element after the fname input element. Here's how the entire table row will look:

```
<tr>
    <td width="116"
align="right"><label
for="fname">First
Name</label></td>
    <td width="283"
align="left"><input name="fname"
type="text" class="inputboxreq"
id="fname" size="30"
onchange="validateField(this,
'fnameErrDisplay');" /></td>
    <td width="242" align="left"
id="fnameErrDisplay"> </td>
</tr>
```

Validating Your Forms *(continued)*

Add `id` attributes to the `td` elements after `lname`, `address`, `city`, `state`, `zcode`, and `email` elements. (Remember the naming convention I am using: `id` of the input element followed by `ErrDisplay`.)

Because I'm not validating the `phone`, `company`, and `address2` fields, I don't need to worry about adding `id` values for the `td` elements after them.

❻ Add an `onsubmit` handler to the form.

An `onsubmit` event for a form triggers a JavaScript routine before the form is submitted. Any event handler you attach to `onsubmit` is your final chance to validate data before the form is processed.

Add the following code inside your `form` element's definition:

```
onsubmit="return
validateAllFields()"
```

This event triggers a JavaScript routine called `validateAllFields()`, which I define shortly. The function returns a Boolean value to the form. If `true`, the form will continue processing; if `false`, the form cancels the submittal process to allow the user to correct errors.

❼ Define the `validateAll Fields()` function.

The `onsubmit` handler that you set up in Step 6 called a JavaScript function named `validateAllFields()`.

You need to define the `validateAll Fields()` function inside a `script` element in the document head.

Here's the code:

```
<script type="text/javascript"
language="JavaScript1.2"
charset="utf-8">
  function validateAllFields( ) {
    var errcount=0;
    // Check all required fields
before submitting the form
    if ( !checkEmail (
document.forms.subform.email,
'emailErrDisplay' ) ) errcount +=
1;
    if ( !checkZipCode ( document.
forms.subform.zcode,
'zcodeErrDisplay' ) ) errcount +=
1;
    if ( !checkState
(document.forms.subform.state,
'stateErrDisplay' ) ) errcount +=
1;
    if ( !checkRequired
(document.forms.subform.city,
'cityErrDisplay' ) ) errcount +=
1;
    if ( !checkRequired
(document.forms.subform.address,
'addressErrDisplay' ) ) errcount
+= 1;
    if ( !checkRequired
(document.forms.subform.lname,
'lnameErrDisplay' ) ) errcount +=
1;
    if ( !checkRequired
(document.forms.subform.fname,
'fnameErrDisplay' ) ) errcount +=
1;
// If any errors are encountered,
alert message is displayed.
Because you are
// also tracking the total number
of errors, you could provide
additional details
// if desired.
    if ( errcount > 0 ) alert(
'One or more problems were
encountered on the data you
entered. Please correct and try
again.' );
// Provide a true/false value
back to the form based on the
results of the routine.
    return ( errcount == 0 );
  };
</script>
```

Validating Your Forms *(continued)*

Note: Make sure this `script` block appears *after* the `formvalidate.js` reference that you added in Step 3.

The `validateAllFields()` function is called when a visitor clicks the Submit button on the form. If a data entry error is discovered, this routine catches the first instance found and displays a message box indicating the problem (see figure on the right). The visitor clicks the OK box to return to the form and correct the mistake.

8 **Save your changes.**

Choose File⇔Save is all you need to do.

9 **Test your form makeover.**

Try previewing the page in your browser by clicking the Preview/Debug In Browser button in the Document toolbar. Then select the desired browser from the list and your Web page is opened for you to test your validation code. Each validation field is checked when you change the data. They are also checked as a group when you click the Submit button.

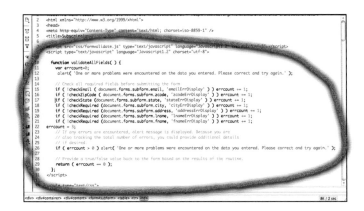

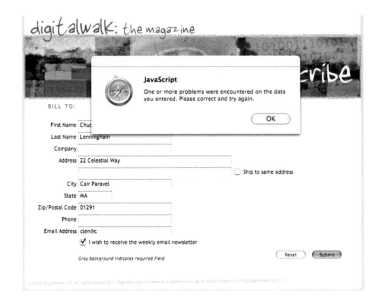

Controlling Tab Order

By default, the tab order of a form is based on the order in which the form elements appear in the source code, which means the order mirrors the pattern you see here to the right. (See the form to the right.) However, this default scheme can be limiting. You may, for instance, wish to tweak the sequence in which the fields are tabbed into throughout the form. Additionally, there may be certain elements that you want to exclude from the tab sequence altogether.

Here's how to control the tab order of your form by using the `tabindex` attribute.

❶ Open an HTML file that contains a form you wish to modify.

For this makeover, feel free to start with `makeover_10_02.html`.

I want to make two tweaks to the tab order to provide a natural flow for the visitor as he or she moves through the form fields. To begin, I want the Ship to Same Address check box to be tabbed into after leaving the Email Address field rather than in its default order — after the second address field. Secondly, I want to remove both the Newsletter check box and the Reset button from the tab order altogether.

❷ View the HTML code of the file.

In Dreamweaver, you do this by clicking the Code button on the Document toolbar.

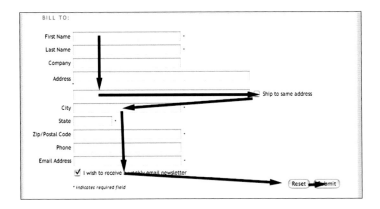

When you are inside the HTML code of your file, navigate to the form you want to customize.

For the book example, look for the form named subform.

③ Add a `tabindex` attribute to the element that you would like to appear first in your tab sequence.

Click your mouse inside the input element with an id of fname. Type tabindex ="1" as a new attribute. The element will look like this:

```
<input name="fname" type="text"
id="fname" size="30"
tabindex="1" />
```

④ Add an incremental `tabindex` value to the rest of the elements in your tab sequence.

Update the rest of the elements in your form, assigning an incremental tabindex value based on the order in which you wish them to be tabbed into.

Note: With the tabindex attribute, form navigation starts with the lowest positive integer and finishes with the highest value. The values do not need to be sequential.

For the book example, I assigned the elements the following tabindex values: lname (2), company (3), address (4), address2 (5), city (6), state (7), zcode (8), phone (9), email (10), shipaddress (11), and submitbutton (12).

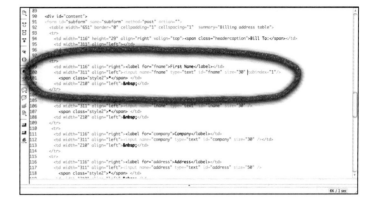

➤ Elements with a tabindex > 0 are selected in increasing order.

➤ Elements with a tabindex = 0 are selected in the order in which they appear in the source file.

➤ Elements with a tabindex < 0 are left out of the tabbing order.

Controlling Tab Order *(continued)*

⑤ Add a negative `tabindex` **value for all elements you don't wish to include in the tab sequence.**

Note: For most browsers (including Internet Explorer), elements with negative `tabindex` attributes are ignored in the tab ordering scheme. For other browsers (Firefox 1.x, for example), you still tab into negative tab indexes, but only after the positive values are completed.

I added `tabindex="-1"` to both the `newsletter` check box and the `resetbutton` elements.

⑥ Save your changes.

Your form now has a tabbing sequence that is based on usability, not on the source code.

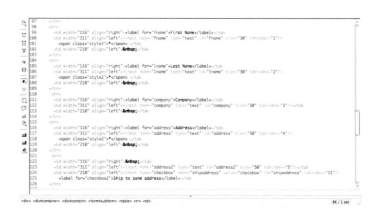

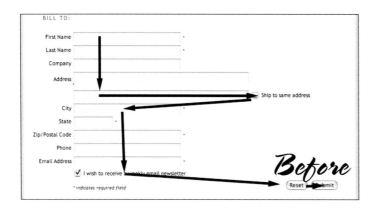

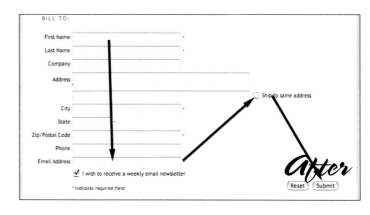

Using CSS to Transform the Look of Form Elements

Until CSS came along, forms were always the ugliest part of most any Web site. (Need some hard evidence? Check out the Web page to the right.) You could work hard to control the look of your text, images, and layout, but when it came to forms and their elements, you were left with squat for formatting options.

You see in Chapter 5 how you can use CSS to alter the look of your text. Fortunately, you can also use CSS to transform the appearance of your forms. The result: forms no longer need be the ugliest parts of your site, but can take on the exact look and feel you want to give them. Here's how:

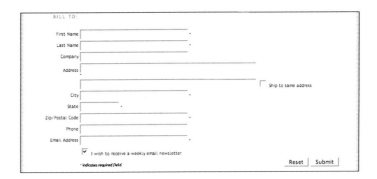

❶ Open an HTML file that contains a form you wish to modify.

If you are following along with my examples, open `makeover_10_03.html`.

In this example, I want to modify the border and font attributes of the form elements so they coordinate with the rest of my Web site styles. In addition, instead of placing asterisks after required fields, I would like to denote required elements with a gray background.

❷ View the HTML code of the file.

Again, in Dreamweaver, you do this by clicking the Code button on the Document toolbar.

Using CSS to Transform the Look of Form Elements *(continued)*

After you are inside the HTML code of your file, move your text cursor into the head element.

③ Add a new `style` element inside the document head.

You can do so by entering the following code anywhere inside your head element:

```
<style type="text/css">
</style>
```

④ Add a CSS rule for each of the form element groupings.

You can define the CSS styles here that you'll attach to your form elements.

For the book example, I define three class styles: `.button` for the two button elements, `.inputbox` for optional text field elements, and `.inputboxreq` for required text fields. Here's the CSS code to insert in the `style` element:

```
.button {
  margin             :  5px 5px
5px 5px;
  padding            : 1px;
  font               : 10px
Trebuchet MS, Arial, Helvetica,
sans-serif;
  font-weight        : bold;
  color              : #999999;
  background-color   : #F3F3F3;
  border             : 1px solid
#CCCCCC;
```

```
 71
 72  .button {
 73    margin              :  5px 5px 5px 5px;
 74    padding             : 1px;
 75    font                : 10px Trebuchet MS, Arial, Helvetica, sans-serif;
 76    font-weight         : bold;
 77    color               : #999999;
 78    background-color     : #F3F3F3;
 79    border              : 1px solid #CCCCCC;
 80    width               : 60px;
 81    height              : 20px;
 82  }
 83
 84  .inputbox {
 85    font                : 11px Trebuchet MS, Arial, Helvetica, sans-serif;
 86    font-weight         : normal;
 87    border-style        : solid;
 88    background-color    : White;
 89    border              : 1px solid #CCCCCC;
 90    padding: 2px;
 91    margin              : 1px 0px 1px 0px;
 92  }
 93
 94  .inputboxreq {
 95    font                : 11px Trebuchet MS, Arial, Helvetica, sans-serif;
 96    font-weight         : normal;
 97    border-style        : solid;
 98    background-color    : #F3F3F3;
 99    border              : 1px solid #CCCCCC;
100    padding: 2px;
101    margin              : 1px 0px 1px 0px;
102  }

<body>                                                                    6K / 1 sec
```

```
   width              : 60px;
   height             : 20px;
}
.inputbox {
    font                   : 11px
Trebuchet MS, Arial, Helvetica,
sans-serif;
        font-weight        : nor-
mal;
        border-style : solid;
    background-color : White;
    border             : 1px solid
#CCCCCC;
    padding: 2px;
    margin             :  1px 0px
1px 0px;
}
.inputboxreq {
    font                   : 11px
Trebuchet MS, Arial, Helvetica,
sans-serif;
        font-weight        : nor-
mal;
        border-style : solid;
    background-color : #F3F3F3;
    border             : 1px solid
#CCCCCC;
    padding: 2px;
    margin             :  1px 0px
1px 0px;
}
```

For each of the elements, the style
defines the font, border, margin, and
padding details appropriate for the element.

Rich's Take: If you are using
Dreamweaver, you can also use the CSS
Styles Panel to define CSS rules through a
series of dialog boxes. View the panel by
choosing Window⇨CSS Styles.

Using CSS to Transform the Look of Form Elements *(continued)*

⑤ Add a `class` **attribute to each of your form elements and associate the desired CSS style to the element.**

For my example, begin by adding `class="inputboxreq"` to the `fname` element:

```
<input name="fname" type="text"
class="inputboxreq" id="fname"
size="30" />
```

Add the same class attribute for the `lname`, `address`, `city`, `state`, and `email` elements.

For the `company`, `address2`, and `phone` elements, add a `class="inputbox"` attribute.

For the `resetbutton` and `submitbutton` elements, insert a `class="button"` attribute into their element definitions.

⑥ Save your changes.

Your form now reflects the CSS attribute settings you specified.

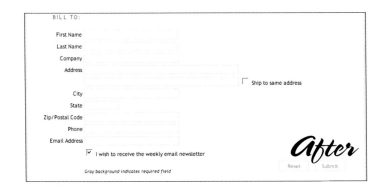

Creating Graphical Buttons

Another favorite makeover for forms involves getting rid of the built-in buttons altogether (see the boring buttons on the page to the right) and using graphical buttons instead. When this is done correctly, you can give an added dose of professionalism to your forms.

To do this makeover, you first create the buttons in Photoshop and then add them into your HTML file in Dreamweaver.

Here's how to create your own graphical buttons:

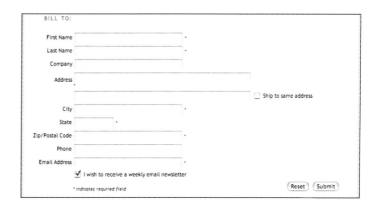

❶ In Photoshop, create a new document (300 x 300 pixels, 72 pixels/inch, transparent background).

Using a transparent background will enable your buttons to look good regardless of the background color of your Web page.

❷ Create a new layer by choosing Layer⇨New⇨Layer.

Name the layer Button in the New Layer dialog box and click OK.

❸ Choose the Rounded Rectangle tool from the tools palette.

The Rounded Rectangle is the best tool in Photoshop for shaping great-looking Web buttons.

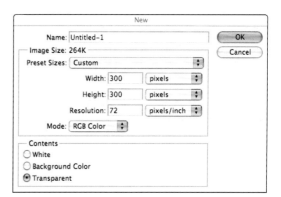

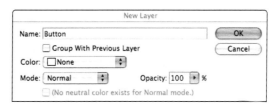

Creating Graphical Buttons *(continued)*

④ In the Options bar for the tool, enter the amount of corner curve you want in the Radius field.

The Radius property sets the amount of curve used in the rounded corners. 6px here gives you a nice look.

⑤ Draw a rounded rectangle 90 x 25 pixels in size.

You can adjust the width and height to meet your specific needs, but 90 x 25 pixels is a good size to start with.

⑥ Tweak the gradient settings for the rounded rectangle.

Access the Gradient Overlay settings by choosing Blending Options from the Layer palette pop-up menu with the Button layer selected. Doing so activates the Layer Style dialog box.

Click the Gradient Overlay check box in the Style list. Next, click the Gradient Overlay text. When you do so, the dialog box is updated to display the Gradient Overlay properties.

Double-click the Gradient drop-down box to activate the Gradient Editor. Here's where you set the left and right color stops and add a new stop at the midpoint. (A *stop* is a point at which the color changes.)

You now want to define the different tones of gray to be used in the gradient.

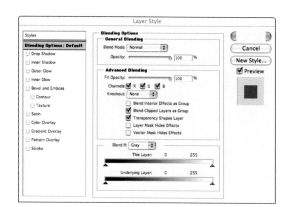

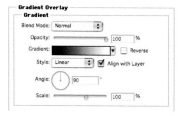

Starting with the bottom-left color stop, double-click it and enter `e1e1e1` in the hex code box of the Color Picker dialog box that appears. Double-click the bottom-right color stop and enter `dadada` as the color code.

Add a new intermediate color stop by clicking the area just below the diamond-shaped midpoint marker. Double-click the color stop and enter `ffffff` in the hex code box of the Color Picker dialog box.

Close out the Gradient Editor by clicking OK. Click OK again to close out of the Layer Style dialog box.

❼ While pressing ⌘ (Ctrl in Windows), click the Button layer in the Layers palette.

The layer dimensions are selected. You'll use the selection to help easily create a border in the following steps.

❽ Create a new layer by choosing Layer⇨New⇨Layer.

Name the layer `ButtonBorder` in the New Layer dialog box and click OK.

❾ Choose Select⇨Modify⇨ Expand.

Enter 1 in the Expand By box and click OK.

❿ Select the Paint Bucket tool from the toolbox.

In the tool's Options bar, make sure the Fill option is set to Foreground and your Foreground color is set to white (#ffffff).

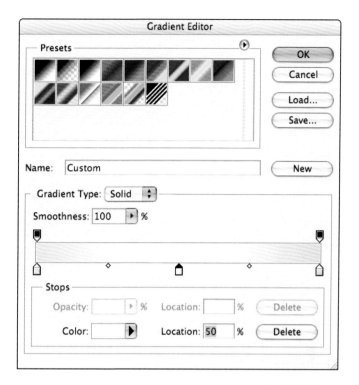

Creating Graphical Buttons *(continued)*

⑪ Click anywhere in the selection.

The Paint Bucket tool fills in the contents of the selection with white.

⑫ Modify the stroke settings of the layer.

Access the Stroke settings by double-clicking the ButtonBorder layer in the Layers palette. The Layer Style dialog box is displayed.

Click the Stroke check box in the Styles list to see the Stroke settings. Change the Size to 1 px, double-click the Color box, and enter b4b3b3 as the hex code color.

Click OK to close the Layer Style dialog box.

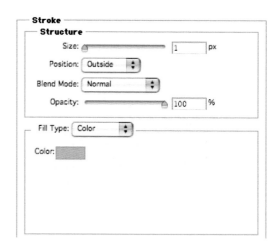

⑬ Move the ButtonBorder layer beneath the Button layer in the Layers palette.

The button look is now complete.

⑭ Save your working file.

Save the entire document as a Photoshop .psd file (webbutton_canvas.psd). You can treat this as your working file for creating Web buttons.

After you have saved the entire workspace, you are ready to copy just the button itself into a separate file.

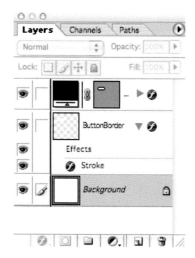

⑮ Choose Select➪Modify➪ Expand.

Enter 1 in the Expand By box and click OK.

⑯ Choose Edit➪Copy Merged.

The visible selection, which includes both layers, is copied as a single graphic to the Clipboard.

⑰ Choose File➪New.

Stick with the defaults (84 x 27 pixels, 72 pixels/inch, RGB Color mode, and Transparent background).

⑱ Choose Edit➪Paste.

The button image is pasted onto the blank canvas.

⑲ Save your image.

Save your image as a Photoshop .psd file under the name webbutton.psd.

⑳ Choose the Horizontal Type tool from the toolbox.

Set the font to Myriad (or Trebuchet MS), 11 point size, Smooth anti-aliasing, and the color to Black (#000000).

㉑ Type Submit.

If you need to reposition the text after entering it, choose the Move tool from the toolbox and center the text layer inside the button.

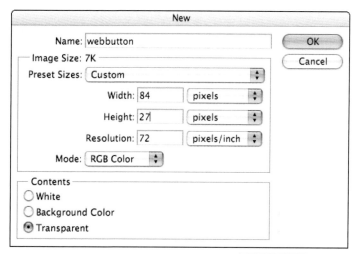

Creating Graphical Buttons *(continued)*

㉒ Choose File⇨Save for Web.

Save the file in GIF format under the name `submitbutton.gif`.

㉓ Repeat Steps 20 through 22 for the Reset button.

Save the GIF image as `resetbutton.gif`.

㉔ Open an HTML file that contains a form you wish to modify.

For this makeover, you may want to start with `makeover_10_04.html`.

I am going to replace the existing HTML buttons in the book example page with graphic buttons.

㉕ In your HTML editor, call up both the Design and Code views.

In Dreamweaver, you do this by clicking the Split button on the toolbar.

㉖ Click the Submit button in Design view.

The element is selected in both the Design and Code views.

㉗ In Code view, replace the Submit Button code.

Replace the Submit Button code with the following:

```
<input type="image"
src="images/submitbutton.gif"
name="submitbutton" alt="Submit
button" />
```

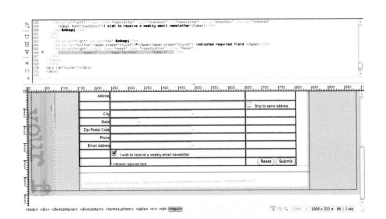

㉘ Click the Reset button in Design view.

The Code view highlights the Reset Button code.

㉙ In Code view, replace the Reset Button code.

While replacing an HTML Submit button with an image equivalent involves just a couple attribute changes, a graphical Reset button is a little trickier. You need to resort to a little JavaScript to do so. Here's the code you replace the original code with to simulate a reset button:

```
<img
src="images/resetbutton.gif"
onclick="javascript:document.sub
form.reset();return false;"
alt="Reset button" />
```

㉚ Save your changes.

Your makeover is complete.

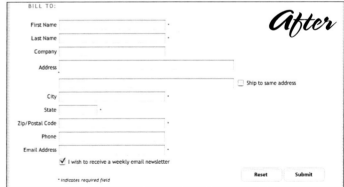

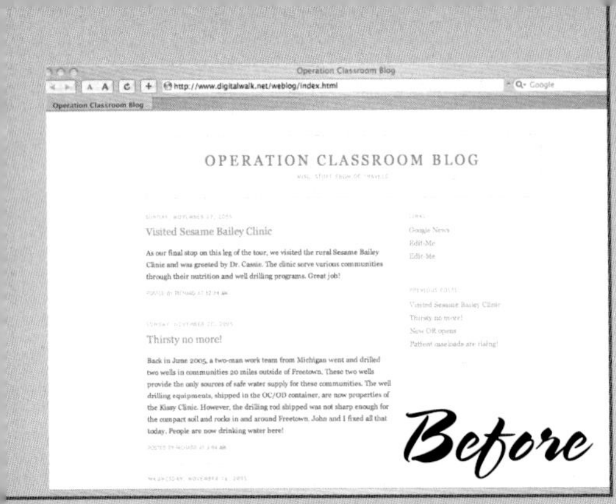
Operation Classroom Blog
http://www.digitalwalk.net/weblog/index.html
OPERATION CLASSROOM BLOG
Visited Sesame Bailey Clinic
Thirsty no more!
Before

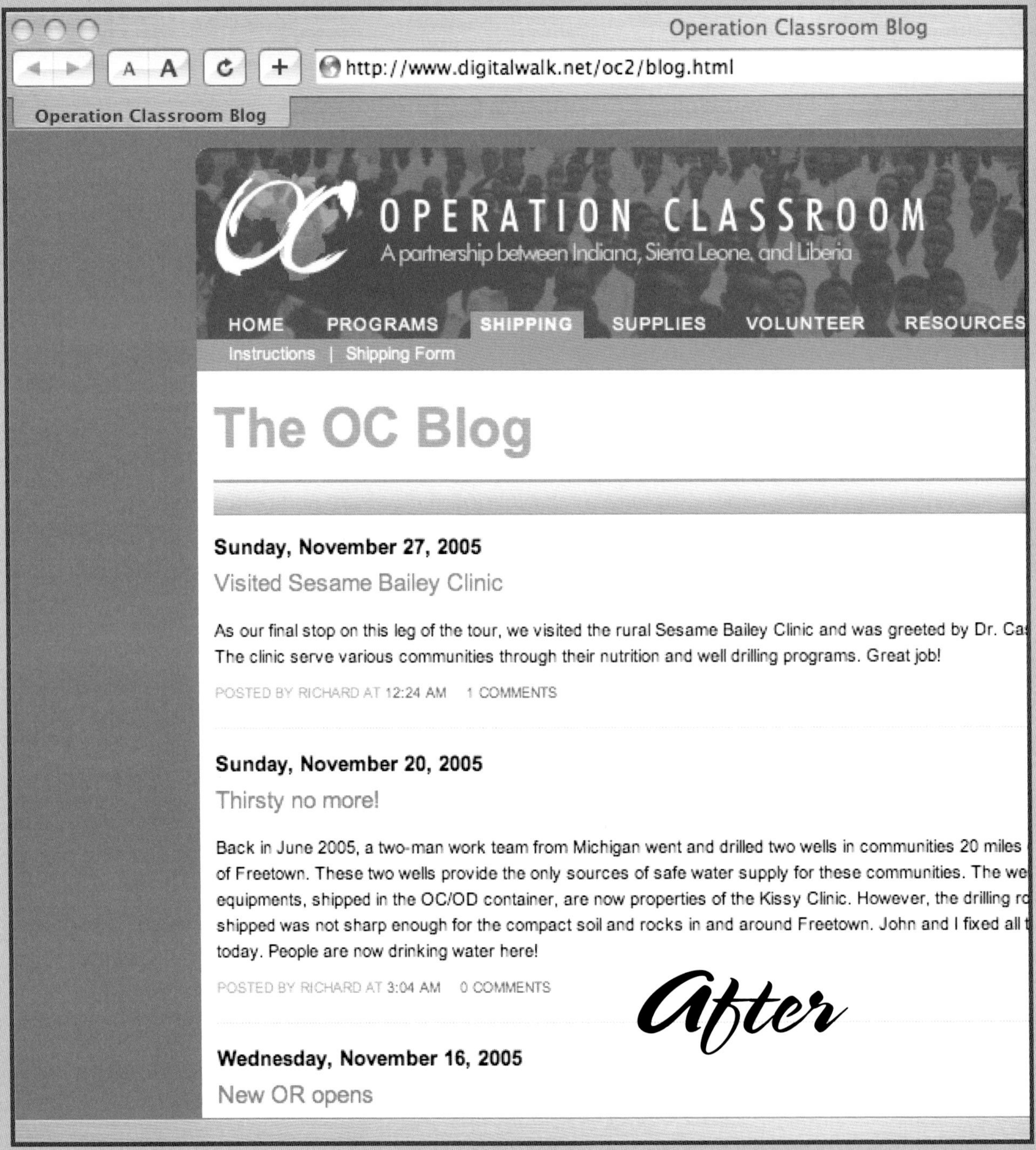
Operation Classroom Blog
http://www.digitalwalk.net/oc2/blog.html
Operation Classroom Blog
OPERATION CLASSROOM
A partnership between Indiana, Sierra Leone, and Liberia
HOME
PROGRAMS
SHIPPING
SUPPLIES
VOLUNTEER
RESOURCES
Instructions | Shipping Form
The OC Blog
Sunday, November 27, 2005
Visited Sesame Bailey Clinic
As our final stop on this leg of the tour, we visited the rural Sesame Bailey Clinic and was greeted by Dr. Ca
The clinic serve various communities through their nutrition and well drilling programs. Great job!
POSTED BY RICHARD AT 12:24 AM 1 COMMENTS
Sunday, November 20, 2005
Thirsty no more!
Back in June 2005, a two-man work team from Michigan went and drilled two wells in communities 20 miles
of Freetown. These two wells provide the only sources of safe water supply for these communities. The we
equipments, shipped in the OC/OD container, are now properties of the Kissy Clinic. However, the drilling r
shipped was not sharp enough for the compact soil and rocks in and around Freetown. John and I fixed all
today. People are now drinking water here!
POSTED BY RICHARD AT 3:04 AM 0 COMMENTS
After
Wednesday, November 16, 2005
New OR opens

11

ADD-ON MAKEOVERS

*I*t's time to bring in the "big boys."

Throughout this book, you've made your way through a bunch of do-it-yourself makeovers designed to transform your Web site. However, you'll eventually encounter a need that you can't pull off using a Web page editor like Dreamweaver (or an image editor like Photoshop) alone. In these circumstances, you need to bring in the "big boys" and get Google, Yahoo!, and other major Web companies to help you make your Web site even better.

In this chapter, I walk you through three makeovers that show you how to integrate Web-based "add-on" services into your Web site. You begin by adding a Yahoo! map and directions link to your site to help your visitors easily locate you in the real world. You then explore a makeover that adds a Google-driven site search to your site. Finally, you look at how you can transform your blog and make it feel like part of your Web site design.

You can always link to services on the Web. The trick is being able to seamlessly integrate (or come as close as possible) these services into your overall visual design to ensure a positive and unmuddied user experience.

Adding Maps and Directions

If you are using your Web site to lead visitors to your physical location, you'll want to go beyond the kind of printed text-based directions you see in the Web page to the right. Although text-based directions can be helpful to some people, others want to see a visual map of your location. Still others want to get directions from their doorstep to yours.

Here's a makeover to add a map and directions to your site.

Note: I base this makeover on Yahoo! Maps. However, you can get similar functionality from other map providers, such as MapQuest and Google. As always, be sure to check with these providers concerning the latest terms and conditions in which they permit their maps to be placed on your Web site.

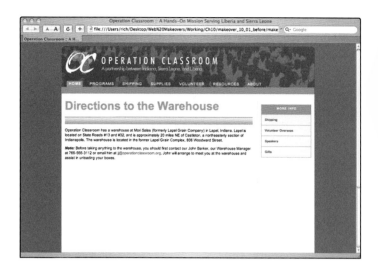

① In your Web page editor of choice, open the HTML file to which you'd like to add a map or directions.

In Dreamweaver, you choose File↪Open. In the Open dialog box, select your file and click Open.

If you are following along with the book's example, open `makeover_11_01.html`.

② If you're using Dreamweaver, click the Split button on the Document toolbar.

You can now view both the Design and Code views of the HTML file.

Go ahead and hide Dreamweaver for now. In Mac OS X, press ⌘+H. In Windows, press the Minimize button on the application title bar.

③ Point your browser to `http://maps.yahoo.com`.

Remember, you can use Google or MapQuest here as well.

④ Enter your address information into the boxes provided and click the Get Map button.

Yahoo! Maps generates a map based on the information you submit.

⑤ Click the Small Map link on the left side of the map.

Yahoo displays a smaller map that is the perfect size for a Web site.

⑥ Right-click the small map and save the image to your local drive.

Put the .GIF image file in the `images` subfolder of your Web site.

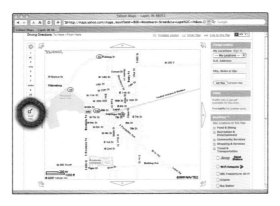

⑦ If you want to include driving directions, click the Link to This Map link.

If you don't want to include driving directions, skip to Step 9.

A new page is shown containing the necessary information for linking to the Yahoo! Maps map.

⑧ Select the HTML code in the Driving Directions box and choose Edit⇨Copy.

After you have the HTML code on the Clipboard, you can minimize your browser and return to Dreamweaver.

⑨ In Dreamweaver, position your cursor where you wish to insert the map in the Design pane.

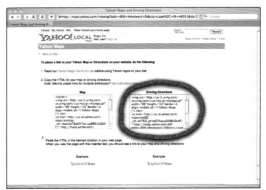

Adding Maps and Directions *(continued)*

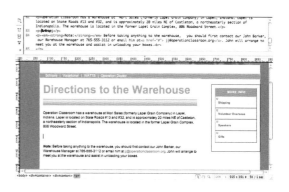

⑩ Choose Insert➪Image.

Doing so calls up the Select Image Source dialog box. Choose the map image that you saved from the Yahoo! Maps Web site and click Choose.

Depending on your Dreamweaver settings, the Image Tag Accessibility Attributes dialog box should show up next.

⑪ Enter alternate text for the map in the Image Tag Accessibility Attributes dialog box and click OK.

You may wish to enter `Map to Our Location`, or something like that.

⑫ Click to select the image and then click the Align Center button in the Properties palette that appears.

Or, if you like right-clicking, right-click and choose Align➪Center from the pop-up menu. Either action centers the image.

Your image is now in place, but if you decided back in Step 8 to copy the driving directions to your location, you still have something on your Clipboard to deal with.

⑬ In the Code pane, position your text cursor where you want to add the link to Yahoo! Directions.

⑭ Choose Edit➪Paste.

The driving directions code you copied back in Step 8 is inserted into your HTML file, just below your map.

⑮ Make any necessary text edits to your page.

If you previously had written directions, you may wish to remove them at this time.

⑯ Save your changes.

In Dreamweaver, choose File➪Save.

⑰ Preview your new map and directions in your browser.

Choosing File➪Preview in Browser and then choosing your desired browser does the trick in Dreamweaver.

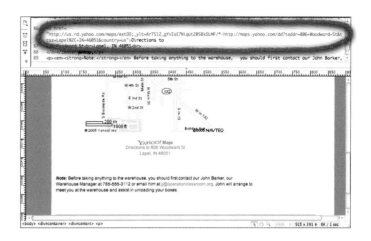

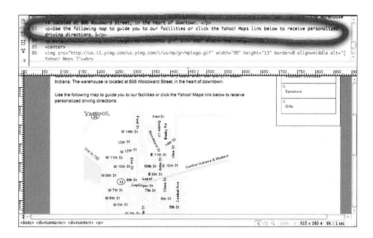

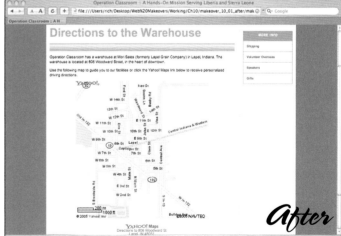

Adding a Site Search

Google and other search engines on the Web are so wildly popular because they provide a way to easily and quickly find information that visitors are searching for. Therefore, when visitors come to your site, they'll be looking for similar functionality and will get frustrated if they have to traverse your navigation menu in search of what they are looking for.

If you'd like to add site search capabilities to your Web site, follow the steps below.

Note: The old adage, "you get what you pay for," certainly applies to site search services. Most free site search offerings from Google and other companies don't allow you to seamlessly integrate the service into your overall visual design. However, if you want to pay, paid services allow you to fully customize the search results.

① Using your Web page editor of choice, open an HTML file to which you would like to add a search box.

In Dreamweaver, you choose File↪Open, select the file from the Open dialog box, and then click Open.

Alternatively, you can create a new page that is specifically designated as your search page.

② Click the Split button on the Document toolbar.

You can now view both the Design and Code views of the HTML file.

Minimize the Dreamweaver window and go to your browser.

❸ Point your browser to `www.google.com/services/free.html`.

This page is your entry point for Google's free customizable SiteSearch service.

❹ Click the Customize Google for Your Site button and follow on-screen instructions to customize the search for your Web site.

You can, for example, specify the text and link colors and background.

Rich's Take: Be sure to use your banner graphic as the URL of your logo. This is your best chance for customizing the search results page.

❺ Click the Update button.

Google displays the HTML code that you'll add to your search page.

❻ Select the HTML code and choose Edit⇨Copy from the browser menu.

It's time to return to Dreamweaver.

❼ In Dreamweaver's Design pane, position your text cursor where you'd like to add the search box.

❽ In the Code pane, match up your text cursor to your current location in the Design pane.

❾ Choose Edit⇨Paste.

Your Google search box code is inserted into your HTML file at the cursor position.

Adding a Site Search *(continued)*

Rich's Take: You may wish to update the default text that Google gives you inside the search box with more user-friendly wording. For example, instead of "Search WWW," I replaced the text with "Search Web." I also replaced "Search www.operationclassroom. org" with "Search Operation Classroom."

⓾ Save your changes.

Don't forget to choose File⇨Save and make those changes permanent.

⓫ Preview your new site inside your browser.

Choose File⇨Preview in Browser in Dreamweaver to display the current page in your default browser.

When you perform a search on your site, the service displays results in a familiar Google-looking format. If you specified a logo, it appears at the top of the page.

Note: Unfortunately, with the free search, Google does not provide a way for users to return to your Web site apart from clicking a link from their search results or by clicking the Back button in their browser.

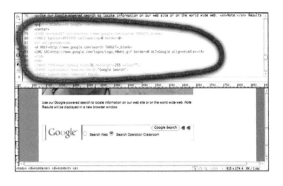

Before

After

Making Your Blog Part of Your Web Site

If Web sites led the Internet revolution during the 1990s, blogs have become the phenomenon of this decade. They're everywhere. Chances are, you already have one or else would like to have one. Blogs are a great way to communicate tidbits of information to people and do so in a manner that is easy for you: updating via e-mail or a browser-based service rather than constantly updating a page in Dreamweaver and publishing the results.

If you'd like to have a blog as part of your Web site, the trick is to start with a blog service and then make its cookie-cutter blog feel less like some foreign body trapped in your Web site (see the blog page to the right) and more like something that seamlessly fits in with the rest of your design.

Here's a way to do it using Blogger, a free service from Google.

Note: If you've not yet signed up with Blogger and configured your blog, press the Pause button and take a moment to do so before continuing.

Important: Blogger lets you choose the directory and filename (Blog URL, FTP path, and Blog filename) on your Web site that the blog is published to. This makeover assumes that the HTML file you specify (e.g., `blog.html`) is in the same directory on your Web server as your other Web site files. If you place it elsewhere, make sure you update your relative links, converting them to absolute URLs.

① In your Web page editor of choice, prepare a new HTML file based on your visual site design.

You can either start from scratch or, better yet, make a copy of an existing page and then strip out the content.

Making Your Blog Part of Your Web Site *(continued)*

Throughout this makeover, I assume you are using the `div`-based layout approach as defined in Chapter 2.

❷ Save your file as `blogger_template.html`.

In Dreamweaver, choose File⇨Save As and save the file in the Save As dialog box.

❸ In Dreamweaver, click the Code button on the Document toolbar.

Throughout this makeover, you'll be adding several bits of code that Blogger uses to add content to the page. So be ready to roll up your sleeves and work with the HTML code.

❹ In the document head, replace your existing title with `<$BlogPageTitle$>`.

Blogger updates this variable when it generates the page with the blog title you specified in the Blogger configuration area.

❺ Add `<$BlogMetaData$>` **in the document head.**

Blogger replaces this variable with the meta data pertaining to your blog.

❻ Add a `style` **element in the document head that defines Blogger-specific rules.**

Type the following code — or else copy and paste it from the `blogger_template.html` file from the Web site associated with this book:

```
<!-- BLOGGER STYLES START HERE -->
<style type="text/css">

/* Posts
-------------------------------
-------------- */
.date-header {
  margin:1.5em 0 .5em;
  }
.post {
```

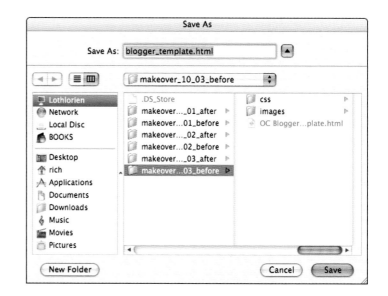

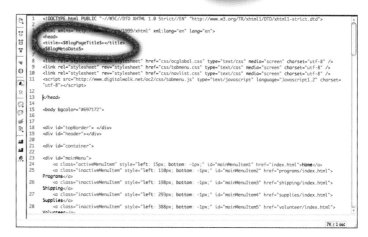

```
   margin:.5em 0 1.5em;
   border-bottom:1px dotted #ccc;
   padding-bottom:1.5em;
   }
.post-title {
   margin:.25em 0 0;
   padding:0 0 4px;
   font-size:140%;
   font-weight:normal;
   line-height:1.4em;
   color:#697172;
   }
.post div {
   margin:0 0 .75em;
   line-height:1.6em;
   }
p.post-footer {
   margin:-.25em 0 0;
   color:#ccc;
   }
.post-footer em, .comment-link {
   font:78%/1.4em Arial,
Helvetica, sans-serif;
   text-transform:uppercase;
   letter-spacing:.1em;
   }
.post-footer em {
   font-style:normal;
   color:#999;
   margin-right:.6em;
   }
.comment-link {
   margin-left:.6em;
   }
.post img {
   padding:4px;
   border:1px solid #ddd;
   }
.post blockquote {
   margin:1em 20px;
   }
.post blockquote p {
   margin:.75em 0;
   }
</style>
<!-- BLOGGER STYLES END HERE -->
```

❼ Scroll down to the content div **element or the location in your document body where you'd like the blog content to be displayed.**

You usually want to add it after the pagetitlespacer div.

Making Your Blog Part of Your Web Site *(continued)*

⑧ Add a heading on your page by updating the content of the `pagetitle` div **element.**

Type `Blog` or something similar.

⑨ Add Blogger-specific XML code inside the `content` div **element, just after** `pagetitle`.

Type the following code or else copy and paste it from the `blogger_template.html` file on the book's Web site:

```
<!-- BLOGGER CODE STARTS HERE -->
<Blogger>

    <BlogDateHeader>
   <h2 class="date-
header"><$BlogDateHeaderDate$></h
2>
   </BlogDateHeader>

   <!-- Begin .post -->
   <div class="post"><a
name="<$BlogItemNumber$>"></a>
         <BlogItemTitle>
      <h3 class="post-title">
        <BlogItemUrl><a
href="<$BlogItemUrl$>"
title="external
link"></BlogItemUrl>
        <$BlogItemTitle$>

<BlogItemUrl></a></BlogItemUrl>
     </h3>
     </BlogItemTitle>

         <div class="post-body">
      <div>
        <$BlogItemBody$>
      </div>
      </div>

      <p class="post-footer">
        <em>posted by
<$BlogItemAuthorNickname$> at <a
href="<$BlogItemPermalinkUrl$>"
title="permanent
link"><$BlogItemDateTime$></a></e
m>

<MainOrArchivePage><BlogItemComme
ntsEnabled>
```

```html
<a class="comment-link"
href="<$BlogItemCommentCreate$>"<
$BlogItemCommentFormOnclick$>><$B
logItemCommentCount$>
comments</a>


</BlogItemCommentsEnabled></MainO
rArchivePage>
<$BlogItemControl$>
     </p>

  </div>
  <!-- End .post -->



  <!-- Begin #comments -->
 <ItemPage>
  <div id="comments">

<BlogItemCommentsEnabled><a
name="comments"></a>

<h4><$BlogItemCommentCount$>
Comments:</h4>
         <dl id="comments-block">
     <BlogItemComments>
     <dt class="comment-poster"
id="c<$BlogCommentNumber$>"><a
name="c<$BlogCommentNumber$>"></a
>
         <$BlogCommentAuthor$>
said...
     </dt>
     <dd class="comment-body">

<p><$BlogCommentBody$></p>
     </dd>
     <dd class="comment-time-
stamp"><a
href="#<$BlogCommentNumber$>"
title="comment
permalink"><$BlogCommentDateTime$
></a>
     <$BlogCommentDeleteIcon$>
     </dd>
     </BlogItemComments>
    </dl>
<p class="comment-timestamp">

    <$BlogItemCreate$>
    </p>
    </BlogItemCommentsEnabled>
<p class="comment-timestamp">
<a href="<$BlogURL$>">&lt;&lt;
Home</a>
    </p>
    </div>
```

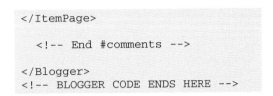

Making Your Blog Part of Your Web Site *(continued)*

```
</ItemPage>

  <!-- End #comments -->

</Blogger>
<!-- BLOGGER CODE ENDS HERE -->
```

⑩ Save changes to your template file.

In Dreamweaver, choosing File⇨Save does this for you.

The local copy of your Blogger template is ready to go. You are now ready to update Blogger with your customized template.

⑪ Choose Edit⇨Select All.

You'll want to get every last bit of code, so be sure to use the Select All command.

⑫ Choose Edit⇨Copy.

With a copy of all your lovely work safely stored on the Clipboard, go ahead and minimize Dreamweaver.

⑬ Point your browser to www. blogger.com and log in.

After logging into Blogger, select your active blog in the Dashboard.

⑭ Click the Template tab.

Doing so displays the area for customizing your current template.

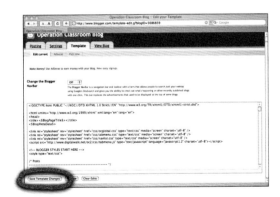

⑮ Select all of the code inside the text box.

The idea here is to mark all the old code for deletion so that the new code can be added.

⑯ Choose Edit⇨Paste.

The existing template code is replaced by your customized template.

⑰ Click the Save Template Changes button.

Doing so saves the template settings for you.

⑱ Click the Republish button to update the blog file on your Web server.

Blogger gets a workout as it updates your blog layout.

⑲ Click the View Blog link to view your newly made-over blog.

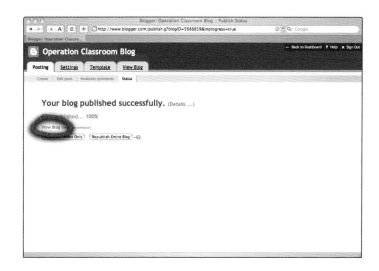

Before

After

Before

After

12

SITE MAKEOVERS

Dot your i's and cross your t's. Go the extra mile. Give it the old college try. Perhaps we'd all jump for joy if these tired old expressions were put out to pasture once and for all. But even if we do get nauseated by them, they do serve as reminders to complete the tasks we're doing without compromising and taking shortcuts.

This chapter explores three makeovers that — here I go — "dot your i's and cross your t's" on your newly transformed Web site. You start out by looking at how to link to other Web sites without shooing away your visitors in the process. Next, I show you how to create and then add one of those nifty Favorites icons to your Web site. As I continue, I walk you through a makeover that optimizes your Web site content for search engines. Finally, I close out by showing you how to quickly convert an HTML page into XHTML, an important markup language standard for the future of the Web.

You can follow along in the chapter by applying the makeovers to your own Web site. However, feel free to work with the HTML files that I highlight in this chapter's makeovers. (As always, they're available for download from the Web site associated with this book.)

Linking to Other Sites without Losing Your Visitors

The Web is built on the hyperlink, forming a bridge from one Web page to another. The beauty of the underlying Web technology is that you can link to a page on your site or on any other site on the planet. The downside is that if you provide a link to another site — like I did on the Web page you see here to the right — visitors may click it and become so absorbed with the new page that they soon forget to ever come back to your site.

Here's how to "have your link and keep visitors, too":

❶ In your HTML editor of choice, open an HTML file that contains a link you wish to modify.

If you want to follow along with my sample files, open `makeover_12_01.html` (available for download from the Web site associated with this book).

If you are working with the page in Dreamweaver, take a moment to be sure you're in Design view. Click the Design button on the Document toolbar, and you'll be there.

❷ In your document body, select the link on your Web page that you wish to make over.

In order to cause the browser to open the link in a new browser window rather than in the existing one, you need to add a `target` attribute to the `link` element.

Once again, the idea here is to help ensure that your page remains open when your visitor checks out another link. You do that by working with multiple browser windows.

Rich's Take: In Dreamweaver, you can modify the target property through the Properties palette. If you are using another HTML editor, you want to find the `a` element in your code.

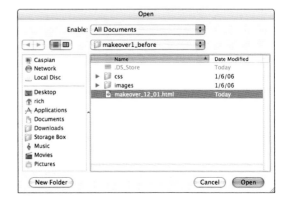

If you are working with the book example, then scroll down to the UNICEF link and position your text cursor inside it.

③ In Dreamweaver, select the _blank value from the Properties palette's Target drop-down list.

The _blank attribute value tells the browser that the target of the link is a brand new browser window.

If you are writing HTML code, add the following to your a element:

```
target="_blank"
```

④ Save your changes.

People say, "save early and often," and they're right.

⑤ Test your link makeover.

You can check out your link makeover in Dreamweaver by choosing File➪Preview in Browser and selecting a browser.

Note: If you are using Firefox, Safari, or another browser that supports tabs, then the new page appears in a separate tab or separate window (depending on your settings). If you are using Internet Explorer, a new browser window appears on top of the original.

Possible target values:

➤ _blank opens the link in a new, blank browser window.

➤ _parent opens the link in the immediate parent of the current frame.

➤ _self opens the link in the same frame as the link.

➤ _top opens the link in the full body of the existing window.

➤ _windowname opens the link in a named frame or iframe element.

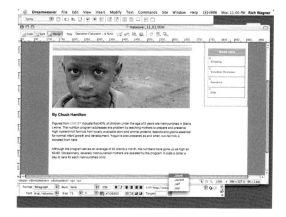

Creating Your Own Favorites Icon

A Favorites icon (or *favicon,* for short) is a tiny graphic that appears next to a Web site's URL in the Address bar of a Web browser. Most Web sites out there have to get by with a white-bread, cookie-cutter graphic imposed upon the viewer by his or her browser of choice, as in the figure to the right. You, however, can do better by creating your own customized favicon for your Web site — just the thing you need to add that professional finishing touch.

The 16-x-16-pixel graphic is saved in a Windows Icon format under the name `favicon.ico`. The `favicon.ico` file is placed on your Web site, usually in the root directory, and then linked to your Web page with a `link` element in the document head.

Here's how to create your own favicon and add it to your Web page. You start by creating the file in Photoshop and then link it to your Web page in Dreamweaver.

❶ Download the ICO Format plug-in for Photoshop.

Photoshop does not provide support for Windows ICO-format graphics out of the box. However, you can download and install a free plug-in from Telegraphics for this purpose. Go to `www.telegraphics.com.au/sw` and download the ICO (Windows Icon) Format plug-in.

❷ Install the plug-in inside your Photoshop Plug-Ins folder.

After the download is complete, unzip the compressed file onto your hard drive. Then copy the `icoformat` file into the File Formats subfolder, which is located in Photoshop's Plug-Ins folder.

Restart Photoshop if you have it opened.

This plug-in adds `.ico` as a supported file extension in your Open and Save dialog boxes.

③ In Photoshop, create a new document (64 x 64 pixels, 72 pixels per inch, transparent background).

While your favicon graphic will need to be 16 x 16, you'll find it easier to design your icon using a 64-pixel square canvas.

④ Design your icon.

The favicon is just 16 x 16 pixels in size, meaning that you have to be very creative with your use of this limited amount of space.

If you would like to use your logo, try opening it in Photoshop and shrinking a rectangular section of it to 16 x 16 pixels. If the size reduction works without making the logo unrecognizable, then your job is done.

If not, then create an icon from scratch by using Photoshop, keeping in mind one basic rule: keep it simple. Surf around some of your favorite Web sites and check out their favicons for examples.

For the sample icon, I stay simple and use only text within the icon. If you are following along, use the Horizontal Type tool and type `d` in the font of your choice. I am using the Jenkins 2.0 typeface, 135 point.

⑤ Save a working version of your favicon image as a Photoshop .psd file.

Before shrinking down the image, be sure to save your larger working version as a `.psd` file first. You'll want to have a working copy on hand in case you ever need to make changes down the line.

If you are using the sample file, save the file as `dw_favicon.psd`.

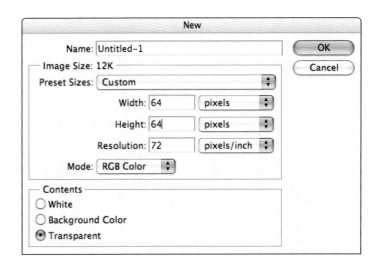

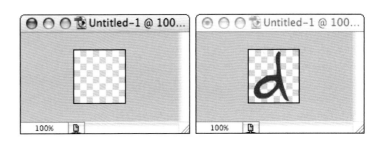

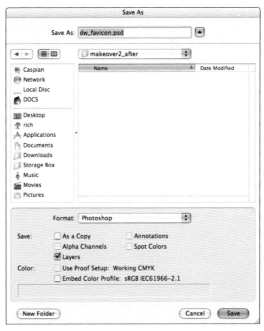

Creating Your Own Favorites Icon *(continued)*

⑥ Shrink the image size to 16 x 16 pixels.

Choose Image⇨Image Size to call up the Image Size dialog box. Enter 16 in the Width and Height boxes and then click OK.

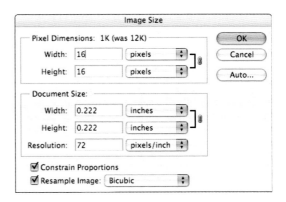

⑦ Save your icon file.

Choose File⇨Save As to display the Save As dialog box.

Save this file in the base directory of your Web site, typically where your home page is located.

Choose ICO (Windows Icon) (*.ICO) from the Format drop-down list. Type `favicon.ico` in the File Name box. Click Save.

⑧ In Dreamweaver, open an HTML file that you'd like to link to your favicon.

Choosing File⇨Open will get you there.

If you are using the example files I've come up with, open `makeover_12_02.html`.

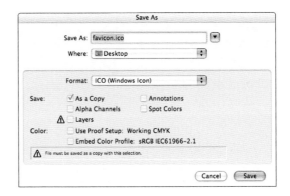

⑨ View the HTML code of the file by clicking the Code button.

You'll associate `favicon.ico` with your Web page by adding code to the document head.

⑩ Add a `link` element to the Web page's document head.

Add a `link` element inside the `head` element as shown below:

```
<link rel="shortcut icon"
href="favicon.ico" />
```

⑪ Save your changes.

You wouldn't want to lose them, would you?

⑫ Test your new Favorites icon.

Choose File⇨View in Browser in Dreamweaver to display the page in your default browser. After the page loads, you'll enjoy your new Favorites icon.

Improving Your Search Engine Ranking

By this point in the book, your Web site is "dressed to kill." But, while the visible part of your Web site is ready, you'll want to be sure and perform one final behind-the-scenes makeover to ensure that your Web site is optimally designed to attract as many visitors as possible.

When a search engine visits your site, it collects various pieces of data from your Web pages, reviews them to determine what search entries are relevant to your site, and decides your overall ranking compared to other sites for those terms.

Each search engine — such as Google, Yahoo!, Alta Vista, and others — indexes and ranks Web sites in a unique way to provide the most relevant results for its users.

Follow these steps to optimize your Web pages for search engines

❶ Open an HTML file that you wish to optimize for search engines.

Choose File➪Open and find your file through the Open dialog box.

❷ Optimize the title of your document.

You probably already know that all browsers use the document title as the window or tab name as well as for Favorites entries. However, the title is also one of the most important pieces of content on your Web page for search engines. All of the search engines factor the document title when they evaluate the Web page. In addition, the title is used as the main entry in the search results listings.

Many factors that determine your ranking are beyond your control (for instance, sites that link to you), but several factors are related to the content of your site, including

> ➤ The title of your page.

> ➤ Meta description and keyword tags in your document head.

> ➤ Use of ALT tags for your images.

> ➤ Keywords appearing within the content of your page.

> ➤ Presence of keywords in your filenames.

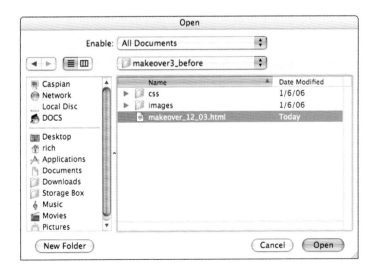

Improving Your Search Engine Ranking *(continued)*

If you are using Dreamweaver, choose Modify➪Page Properties from the menu to display the Page Properties dialog box. Click the Title/Encoding item from the Category list.

In the Title box, enter a descriptive page title and click OK.

If you are using another Web editor, edit the content of the `title` element located inside your document head.

❸ Add a `meta` description tag to your document head.

A `meta` description tag gives you some degree of control over the summary text that is displayed for the page in the search engine listings.

Note: The content in your `meta` description tag matters only for search engines that support it. Google, for example, ignores the tag completely. It generates the summary text automatically based on the content of your Web page.

Rich's Take: A good general rule is to take the first couple of sentences from your Web page's content and use the text as your descriptor.

In Dreamweaver, view the HTML code of the file by clicking the Code button.

Locate the `head` element at the top of your document. Next, inside the document head, add the following tag, replacing the *Add content here* text with your own descriptor:

```
<meta name="description" con-
tent="Add content here">
```

❹ Add a `meta` keywords tag to your document head.

The `meta` keywords tag is another way to tell search engines specific keywords to

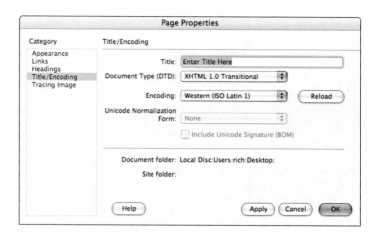

Rich's Take: Keep your title to under 80 characters, but make sure it is expressive enough to adequately describe your page. More importantly, be sure to creatively incorporate specific keywords — the words that people search on — that you'd like your page to be found in search results.

index as they process your Web page. The `meta` keywords tag may sound promising, but don't get too excited. Because they are prone to abuse by Web site designers, most of the major search engines ignore them altogether. However, to account for those engines that do use them, it's good practice to include them.

In Dreamweaver, you should still be inside the document head after Step 3. Next, add a `meta` tag using the model shown below:

```
<meta name="keywords"
content="Add keywords here">
```

⑤ Add `alt` tags to your images.

Search engines use `alt` tags as a way to index the content of your images on your Web page. The use of `alt` tags is particularly important if you have a graphics-heavy home page.

⑥ Save your changes.

You'll rest easier.

⑦ Consider renaming the HTML file to a more descriptive name.

Some search engines use the URL of a Web page as a factor in determining its content. While you wouldn't want to rename the `index.html` file to another name, consider renaming other pages of your site using keywords that best describe each document's contents.

To rename the file, close the file in Dreamweaver and use your normal renaming process in Mac OS X or Windows.

After all that hard work, you should see your Web site inching up the search engines' rankings, as shown here to the right.

Rich's Take: If you use meta keywords on your page, follow three rules: (1) Keep the number of keywords under 20. (2) Don't repeat the same word, even if it appears in multiple key terms. (3) Don't add keywords that don't have anything to do with the content of your Web page.

Converting Your Web Page to XHTML

The Web has always been built on HTML, the markup language that made the Internet into what it is today. However, the Web standards governing body, known as the W3C, has recently recommended a new language specification known as XHTML (*E*xtensible *H*ypertext *M*arkup *L*anguage). If you look at the code itself, XHTML looks very similar to HTML. However, it is a cleaner and better-structured markup language than age-old HTML. Because all future Web changes will focus on XHTML, and because all modern browsers support XHTML, it's a good idea to convert your Web pages to XHTML.

You'll notice that the HTML code in the figure on the right has a mixture of formatting. Some tags are uppercase, while others are lower. Some attribute values are enclosed in quotation marks, while others aren't. While the forgiving HTML has always been nice, it does lead to problems that XHTML is designed to overcome.

The good news is that, if you have Dreamweaver, the transformation process is a snap. Here's how to do this code-based makeover.

❶ Open the HTML file that you'd like to convert to XHTML.

Choose File⇨Open from the menu.

You can use an example file by opening `makeover_12_04.html`.

❷ Choose File⇨Convert⇨XHTML 1.0 Transitional (or XHTML 1.0 Strict) from the menu.

Transitional and Strict are two flavors of XHTML. XHTML Transitional is more forgiving of small code errors; as its name suggests, XHTML Strict is more rigid and limited.

```
1    <HTML>
2    <HEAD>
3    <TITLE>The Music Unplugged :: Tune Powered</TITLE>
4    <META HTTP-EQUIV="Content-Type" CONTENT="text/html; charset=iso-8859-1">
5    <link rel="stylesheet" href="tgu.css" type="text/css">
6
7    <script type="text/javascript" language="Javascript" charset="utf-8">
8
9        if (document.images) { rollovers=1 };
10
11       function rolloverOn( imgName )
12           {if ( rollovers ) { document[imgName].src = eval( imgName + "_on.src" );}}
13
14       function rolloverOff( imgName )
15           {if ( rollovers ) { document[imgName].src = eval( imgName + "_off.src" );}}
16
17   </script>
18
19   </HEAD>
20   <BODY BGCOLOR=#000000 LEFTMARGIN=0 TOPMARGIN=0 MARGINWIDTH=0 MARGINHEIGHT=0>
21   <DIV align="center">
22   <!-- ImageReady Slices (tgu_power.psd) -->
23   <TABLE WIDTH=790 BORDER=0 CELLPADDING=0 CELLSPACING=0>
24       <TR>
25           <TD ROWSPAN=9>
26               <IMG SRC="images/copyright.gif" WIDTH=21 HEIGHT=588 ALT=""></TD>
27
28           <TD COLSPAN=2 ROWSPAN=3> <a href="index.html"><IMG SRC="images/tgubanner.gif" WIDTH=563 HEIGHT=84 ALT="" border="0"></a></TD>
29           <TD COLSPAN=11>
30               <IMG SRC="images/power_03.gif" WIDTH=206 HEIGHT=12 ALT=""></TD>
31       </TR>
32       <TR>
```

`<body>`   6K / 1 sec

Rich's Take: In general, you'll almost certainly want to start off using XHTML Transitional. Before using the more austere option, you will want to fully understand the strict demands of XHTML Strict. For example, XHTML Strict disallows several common elements (such as `iframe`) and forces all formatting to be done via CSS.

```
1  <HTML>
2  <HEAD>
3  <TITLE>The Music Unplugged :: Tune Powered</TITLE>
4  <META HTTP-EQUIV="Content-Type" CONTENT="text/html; charset=iso-8859-1">
5  <link rel="stylesheet" href="tgu.css" type="text/css">
6
7  <script type="text/javascript" language="Javascript" charset="utf-8">
8
9      if (document.images) { rollovers=1 };
10
11     function rolloverOn( imgName )
12        {if ( rollovers ) { document[imgName].src = eval( imgName + "_on.src" );}}
13
14     function rolloverOff( imgName )
15        {if ( rollovers ) { document[imgName].src = eval( imgName + "_off.src" );}}
16
17 </script>
18
19
20 <BODY BGCOLOR=#000000 LEFTMARGIN=0 TOPMARGIN=0 MARGINWIDTH=0 MARGINHEIGHT=0>
21 <DIV align="center">
22 <!-- ImageReady Slices (tgu_power.psd) -->
23 <TABLE WIDTH=790 BORDER=0 CELLPADDING=0 CELLSPACING=0>
24    <TR>
25       <TD ROWSPAN=9>
26          <IMG SRC="images/copyright.gif" WIDTH=21 HEIGHT=588 ALT=""></TD>
27
28       <TD COLSPAN=2 ROWSPAN=3> <a href="index.html"><IMG SRC="images/tgubanner.gif" WIDTH=563 HEIGHT=84 ALT="" border="0"></a></TD>
29       <TD COLSPAN=11>
30          <IMG SRC="images/power_03.gif" WIDTH=206 HEIGHT=12 ALT=""></TD>
31    </TR>
32    <TR>
```
Before

```
1  <!DOCTYPE html PUBLIC "-//W3C//DTD XHTML 1.0 Strict//EN" "http://www.w3.org/TR/xhtml1/DTD/xhtml1-strict.dtd">
2  <html xmlns="http://www.w3.org/1999/xhtml">
3  <head>
4  <title>The Music Unplugged :: Tune Powered</title>
5  <meta http-equiv="Content-Type" content="text/html; charset=ISO-8859-1" />
6  <link rel="stylesheet" href="tgu.css" type="text/css" />
7
8  <script type="text/javascript" charset="utf-8">
9
10     if (document.images) { rollovers=1 };
11
12     function rolloverOn( imgName )
13        {if ( rollovers ) { document[imgName].src = eval( imgName + "_on.src" );}}
14
15     function rolloverOff( imgName )
16        {if ( rollovers ) { document[imgName].src = eval( imgName + "_off.src" );}}
17
18 </script>
19 </head>
20 <body bgcolor="#000000" leftmargin="0" topmargin="0" marginwidth="0" marginheight="0">
21 <div align="center">
22 <!-- ImageReady Slices (tgu_power.psd) -->
23 <table width="790" border="0" cellpadding="0" cellspacing="0">
24    <tr>
25       <td rowspan="9">
26          <img src="images/copyright.gif" width="21" height="588" alt="" /></td>
27
28       <td colspan="2" rowspan="3"> <a href="index.html"><img src="images/tgubanner.gif" width="563" height="84" alt="" border="0" /></a></td>
29       <td colspan="11">
30          <img src="images/power_03.gif" width="206" height="12" alt="" /></td>
31    </tr>
```
After

Before

After

13

EXTREME MAKEOVERS

If you want to get the most out of your Web site, sometimes you have to go to extremes. That's what this chapter is all about.

In this chapter, I show you four makeovers that make your site extremely flexible, user-friendly, and even safe from spammers. You begin with a makeover that enables users to easily adjust the font size of your Web page with a single click — even saving the setting for future visits. Next, one of the dirty tricks of spammers is to scour Web sites for e-mail addresses. I show you a makeover that lets you continue to place your e-mail address on your pages but do so in a way that foils the nasty tricks of the spammers. You then explore a way to personalize your site based on the number of times the visitor has been to your site. Finally, you explore how to add an RSS feed to your Web site.

Allowing Visitors to Adjust the Font Size

Back in Chapter 5, I walk you through a makeover to set your default font. Although my recommendation was to use a smaller font to achieve a more attractive site look — kind of like what you see here on the right — some of your visitors may prefer a larger size.

The following makeover allows you to keep your default font size where you want it for design purposes but allows visitors to use a font sizer box as an easy way to tweak it for their individual needs.

Note: Before beginning this makeover, you should download several files associated with this makeover from the Web site associated with this book. Copy `fontsizer.css` and `fontsizer.js` into the `css` subfolder of your Web site, and copy the four associated `.gif` files — `smallfont.gif`, `medfont.gif`, `largefont.gif`, and `xlfont.gif` — into your images subfolder.

❶ Open an HTML file that you'd like to make over.

Choose File⇨Open in Dreamweaver and select the file from the Open dialog box.

If you're following along with the book examples, you want to work with `makeover_13_01.html`.

Click OK to close out the dialog box and open the Web page.

② **In Dreamweaver, click the Code button on the Document toolbar.**

You see the HTML code for your document.

③ **Link the external stylesheet `fontsizer.css` in the document head of the HTML file.**

The `fontsizer.css` stylesheet, located on the Web site associated with this book, contains the styles associated with the font sizer box. Copy this file to your `css` subfolder and then add the following code inside the `head` element of your document:

```
<link rel="stylesheet"
rev="stylesheet" href="css/font-
sizer.css" type="text/css"
media="screen" charset="utf-8" />
```

④ **Link the external JavaScript library file `fontsizer.js` in the document head of the HTML file.**

The `fontsizer.js` library, available for download from the Web site associated with this book, contains the scripting logic associated with this makeover. Along with `fontsizer.css`, copy this file into the `css` subfolder of your Web site.

Next, to reference it in your HTML file, enter the following code in the `head` element:

```
<script src="css/fontsizer.js"
type="text/javascript" lan-
guage="Javascript1.2"
charset="utf-8"></script>
```

Chapter 13: Extreme Makeovers

Allowing Visitors to Adjust the Font Size *(continued)*

⑤ Locate the spot in your document body where you'd like to add the font sizer box.

If you're working with a `div`-based layout, as shown throughout this book, you'll want to add the font sizer box inside your `rightColumn` `div` element, just under the `navlist` `div`.

This is the same spot you'll want to place your insertion point if you're working with the book example.

⑥ Type or insert the `fontbox` code.

The following HTML code adds the user interface to the font sizer:

```
<!-- START FontSizer -->
<div class="fontbox">
<div class="fontboxcaption">
Adjust Font Size:<br />
<div id= "smallFont"
class="inactiveFontIcon">
<a href="#"
onClick="changeFontSize(65);
return false;"><img
src="images/smallfont.gif"
alt="Small Font" width="16"
height="16" hspace="1" vspace="1"
border="0"></a>
</div>
<div id= "medFont"
class="activeFontIcon">
<a href="#"
onClick="changeFontSize(75);
return false;"><img
src="images/medfont.gif"
alt="Medium Font" width="16"
height="16" hspace="1" vspace="1"
border="0"></a>
</div>
<div id= "largeFont"
class="inactiveFontIcon">
<a href="#"
onClick="changeFontSize(85);
return false;"><img
src="images/largefont.gif"
alt="Large Font" width="16"
height="16" hspace="1" vspace="1"
border="0"></a>
</div>
<div id= "xlFont"
class="inactiveFontIcon">
```

```
68   </div>
69
70   <div id="rightColumn">
71   <img src="images/p2006b.gif" alt="Project 2006 Details" width="150" height="76" style="margin-bottom:1em;">
72
73   <div id="navlist">
74   <h2>Quick Links </h2>
75   <ul>
76   <li><a href="#">Pack&amp;Ship Forms </a></li>
77   <li><a href="#">Volunteer Opportunities </a></li>
78   <li><a href="#">OC Event Info </a></li>
79   <li><a href="#">Download Presentations </a></li>
80   </ul>


86   </h2>
       <img src="images/kids.jpg" width="150" height="62"></p>
87   <p>Operation Classroom is an Indiana-based non-profit organization partnering with selected schools and health care facilties in
       Sierra Leone and Liberia. </p>
88   <p>We seek to: </p>
89   <ul>
90   <li>Partner with Africans to provide first-rate educational system</li>
91   <li>Upgrade the teaching staff</li>
92   <li>Provide educational supplies, equipment, and text books. </li>
93   <li>Help students in need with work study scholarships</li>
94   <li>Work with the Africans to upgrade and construct classroom buildings</li>
95   <li>Help provide emergency relief in war-torn areas of Sierra Leone and Liberia</li>
96   </ul>
```

```
<head>                                                    8K / 2 sec
```

```
<a href="#"
onClick="changeFontSize(95);
return false;"><img
src="images/xlFont.gif"
alt="Extra Large Font" width="16"
height="16" hspace="1" vspace="1"
border="0"></a>
</div>
<script language="JavaScript"
type="text/javascript">setActiveI
con();</script>
</div>
</div>
<!-- END FontSizer -->
```

You can type it in yourself or, better yet, copy and paste it from the `makeover_13_01_after.html` file.

❼ Save changes to your document.

In Dreamweaver, choosing File⇨Save does the trick.

❽ Preview your makeover.

Click the Preview/Debug in Browser button in Dreamweaver and then select a browser from the pop-up menu to display the font sizer box.

❾ Click the font size image buttons to change the size of your body font.

The figures to the right show the Operation Classroom Web site with a small font, large font, and extra-large font.

Scrambling Your E-mail Links to Avoid Spam

One of the old tricks of spammers is to use spider programs to automatically scour Web sites in search of helpless, defenseless e-mail addresses just waiting to be picked up and added to their databases. One of the best ways you can foil spamming attempts is by not printing your e-mail address on your Web site. However, because you want your visitors to be able to contact you via e-mail, here's a makeover for you. This makeover scrambles your e-mail links in the pages on your Web server. However, when loaded inside the browser of an actual visitor, these links are transformed into workable `mailto` links.

❶ Open an HTML file that contains e-mail links that you'd like to scramble.

Choose File➪Open from the Dreamweaver menu. Select the file and click OK.

If you'd like to use an example page, open `makeover_13_02.html`.

Note: I provide two levels of spam protection power for this makeover: The basic level is easy to work with but possible for industrious spammers to account for. A second maximum level is harder to work with but becomes much more difficult for spammers to deal with.

Before you begin this makeover, be sure to download `scramble.js` from the Web site associated with this book and copy it into your `css` subfolder.

❷ Click the Code button on the Document toolbar.

You see the HTML code for your document.

③ Replace your normal e-mail address with a scrambled version.

Choose Edit⇨Find and Replace in Dreamweaver. In the Find and Replace dialog box, enter your normal address in the Find box.

In the Replace dialog box, enter a scrambled e-mail address based on the level of protection you wish to define:

For basic protection, simply replace the @ with _at_. For example, `joe@operationclassroom.org` becomes `joe_at_operationclassroom.org`.

For maximum protection, replace the @ with !a!, replace the period with !d!, and replace the domain suffix with !ds!. For example, `joe@operationclassroom.org` becomes `joe!a!operationclassroom!d!!ds!`

Click Replace All to change all instances of the normal e-mail address into the scrambled equivalent.

④ Scroll down to the bottom of the document body.

The code you'll be adding must be the last thing before the `</body>` end tag.

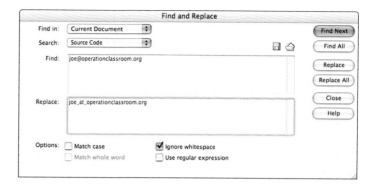

Scrambling Your E-mail Links to Avoid Spam *(continued)*

⑤ Add a reference to the scramble.js JavaScript library file.

The scramble.js file contains the unscrambling routine. Type the following:

```
<script src="css/scramble.js"
type="text/javascript"
language="Javascript1.2"
charset="utf-8"></script>
```

⑥ Add JavaScript code to call the unscramble routine.

Below the script element that references the external file, add a second script element. Inside the element, call the unscramble() JavaScript function based on the following rules:

If you are using the basic level of protection, simply use unscramble(0).

If you are using the maximum level of protection, the call depends on your domain suffix type. If you have a .com suffix, simply type unscramble(1). If you have a suffix other than .com, such as .org, .net, or .edu, then type unscramble(1, domainSuffix). For example, use the following to unscramble the book example: unscramble(1, 'org').

The unscramble() function is called when the page loads, converting all of the scrambled e-mail addresses into normally formatted ones.

⑦ Save changes to your document.

Choose File⇨Save from the menu.

❽ Preview your makeover.

Click the Preview/Debug in Browser button on the Document toolbar in Dreamweaver. Then, select the browser of your choice from the drop-down menu to preview the makeover.

Notice that when you click the `mailto` link in your browser, the properly formatted e-mail address is used.

Advanced Tip: You can modify the symbols used for the maximum protection by opening `scramble.js` inside Dreamweaver and changing the `separator`, `dot`, and `suffix` variables in the `unscramble()` function. However, make sure that the symbols you use in your Web pages match your changes in this JavaScript routine.

With this makeover, spammers will no longer be able to search through the HTML code of your Web site and mine your e-mail address. (Check out the Inboxes below. Which one would you prefer?)

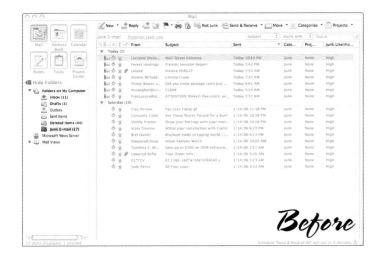

Displaying Different Content Based on the Frequency of the Visitor

You may wish to display or hide content on your Web site depending on the type of visitor. Perhaps you wish to display introductory text for first-time visitors — kind of like what you see here to the right — but prefer to hide this from someone who comes to your site frequently. Or perhaps you'd like to notify your frequent visitors of a special "customer appreciation" sale.

The following makeover shows or hides a `div` element on your page, based on the number of times that the visitor has been to the page before. I divide the visitors into three types: first-time visitors (no previous visits), occasional visitors (1–3 previous visits), and regular visitors (more than 3 visits).

If you're working with the book examples, you will be adjusting the content of the right column in the sample home page (`makeover_03_03.html`), depending on these three visitor types.

Note: Before starting this makeover, be sure to download `user.js` from the Web site associated with this book and copy it into the `css` subfolder of your Web site.

① Open the HTML file that you'd like to personalize.

Choose File⇨Open from the Dreamweaver menu.

② Click the Code button on the Document toolbar.

You see the HTML code for your document.

③ Add a link to the `user.js` JavaScript library file in the document head.

The `user.js` file, available for download from the Web site associated with this book, contains the JavaScript routines that you'll call from your Web page to determine the visibility of a `div` element. Enter the following code:

```
<script src="css/user.js"
type="text/javascript" lan-
guage="Javascript1.2"
charset="utf-8"></script>
```

④ Enclose "first-time visitor" content inside a `div` element with a class of `firstTimerStory`.

If you're working with the book example, add the `div` element around the "Who We Are" block in the right column of the page.

Repeat as desired for any block of text on your page that you'd like to show only for infrequent visitors.

⑤ Enclose "regular" content inside a `div` element with a class of `regularStory`.

For the book example, add the `regular Story` element around the "Join Us at Our Annual Volunteer Appreciation Dinner" block.

Repeat as desired for any content on the page that you'd like reserved for more frequent users.

⑥ Add a call to the JavaScript routine `contentSelector()` **at the end of your document body.**

Locate the `</body>` tag at the end of your document and insert the following code before it:

```
<script language="JavaScript"
type="text/javascript">
contentSelector();
</script>
```

`contentSelector()` is a routine inside the `user.js` library file that displays or hides `firstTimeStory` and `regularStory` class `div` elements depending on the number of times the visitor has come to that page. For first-time visitors, `firstTimeStory` elements are displayed, while the `regularStory` elements are hidden. For occasional visitors, both `firstTimeStory` and `regularStory` elements are shown. Finally, for regular visitors, the `regularStory` elements are displayed, while hiding `firstTimeStory` elements.

⑦ Save changes to your document.

Choose File⇨Save from the menu.

⑧ Preview your makeover.

As always, click the Preview/Debug in Browser button on the Document toolbar. After you select the desired browser from the list, the Web page is displayed.

The content will vary based on the number of times you view the page.

First Time

Occasional

Regular

Adding an RSS Feed to Your Web Site

RSS, which stands for *Really Simple Syndication,* offers an easy way to "syndicate" news on your site. With RSS, you can publish a feed containing the latest news stories, blog entries, or whatever content you consider important. People can subscribe to your feeds and then view this content in an RSS reader or in newer browsers, such as the Live Bookmarks feature of Firefox. These RSS stories are then linked back to your Web site if a person wishes to view further details about it.

An RSS feed — usually denoted by the small, radio-wave-like RSS icon in your browser status bar — allows you to communicate with visitors who are interested in your content when they subscribe to your RSS feed.

The following makeover shows you how to add your own RSS feed to your Web site.

Rich's Take: The RSS feed is contained in an XML document that resides on your Web server. For this makeover, you need to create this new document by hand, following the steps below. If you'd like to create an RSS feed that links to content on your home page, check out the RSS Dreamfeeder, a commercial Dreamweaver extension from RNSoft (www.rnsoft.com).

Note: Download the rss.png file from the Web site associated with this book and put it in your images subfolder before you begin this makeover.

Adding an RSS Feed to Your Web Site *(continued)*

① Open the `rssfeed_template.rss` **file.**

You can find the `rssfeed_template.rss` file on the Web site associated with this book. This XML document provides the document structure that you use to define your own RSS feed.

② Save the template file under a new name, keeping the `.rss` **extension.**

Choose File⇨Save As from the menu. In the Save As dialog box, give the file a new name and click Save.

You'll now fill the content into the XML document.

③ Add a title for your news feed inside the `title` **element.**

If you're working with the book example, enter `Operation Classroom News`.

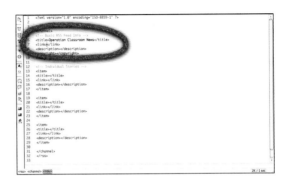

④ Add a URL to your site's home page or news page inside the `link` **element.**

For the book example, latest news is highlighted on the home page, so add a reference to this page.

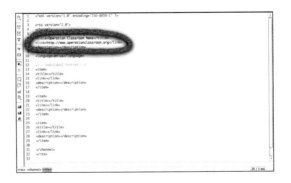

⑤ Add a description of the RSS feed inside the first `description` **element.**

This description is often used by an RSS reader to tell about your feed.

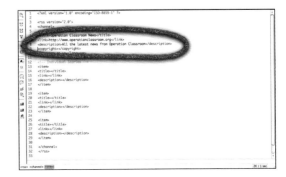

6 Add copyright information inside the copyright element.

Help protect your content by adding some legalese:

```
Copyright ©2006, Operation
Classroom. All Rights Reserved.
```

7 Add news story details inside the first item element.

Each item element contains the details of an RSS news entry: a title of the story, a link to your Web site, and an optional description of the story.

The link content may point to a specific article page or else a named anchor on your home or news page.

Some RSS feeds simply contain a title and a link, prompting users to click the link to view the details of the story. Other feeds display all of the story's text that is placed inside the story's description element.

Rich's Take: If you've already got your news stories written up on your Web page, simply do a quick copy-and-paste operation, inserting the title and story text in the appropriate places in the XML document.

8 Repeat Step 7 for each story that you'd like to include in your RSS feed.

Add any additional item elements that you need.

9 Save changes to your RSS feed document.

Choose File➪Save from the menu.

Your RSS feed is now ready to go. You just need to reference it in your HTML file.

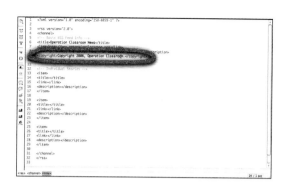

Adding an RSS Feed to Your Web Site *(continued)*

⑩ Open the HTML file that you'd like to link to the RSS feed.

Choose File⇨Open in Dreamweaver and select the appropriate file in the dialog box that appears.

If you're working with the book example, open `makeover_13_04.html`.

⑪ Click the Code button on the Document toolbar.

The HTML code for your file appears.

⑫ Add a `link` element in your document head.

The link element associates the `.rss` file you previously created with this page. Enter the code as follows:

```
<link rel="alternate"
type="application/rss+xml"
title="RSS" href="ocnews.rss" />
```

⑬ Click the Design button in the Document toolbar.

Dreamweaver displays the visual design view of the Web page.

⑭ If your `.rss` file points to named anchors on your page, define named anchors for your articles.

Position the cursor at the start of the article headline and choose Insert⇨Named Anchor from the menu.

The Named Anchor dialog box is displayed. Enter an anchor name, such as story1, and click OK.

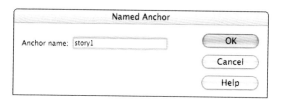

⓯ Scroll down to the bottom of your news section.

You'll add an RSS graphic here.

⓰ Insert the rss.png image into your Web page.

Choose Insert⤷Image from the menu. The Select Image Source dialog box appears. Select the rss.png file from your images subfolder and click Choose or OK.

The image is inserted into your document.

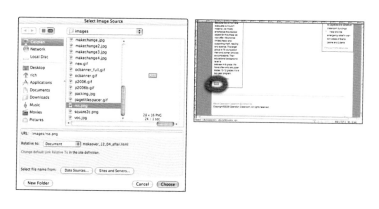

⓱ Select the rss.png image and then add a link to your .rss file in the Properties palette.

⓲ Save changes to your HTML file.

Choose File⤷Save.

⓳ Preview your makeover.

Press F12 in Dreamweaver to display the RSS-enabled Web page in your default browser. If you use Firefox or a browser that provides RSS support, you'll see the RSS notification icon.

Visitors will be able to click the RSS graphic on your page or the browser's RSS icon to subscribe to your feed.

Index